THE AVIAN ARK

THE AVIAN ARK

Tales from a Wild-bird Hospital

Kit Chubb

Hungry Mind Press
Saint Paul, Minnesota

Originally published by Western Producer Prairie Books
Saskatoon, Saskatchewan

First U.S. Edition
Published by Hungry Mind Press
57 Macalester Street
Saint Paul, Minnesota 55105

9 8 7 6 5 4 3 2
First Hungry Mind Press Printing, 1995

Library of Congress Catalog Card Number: 95-079539

ISBN: 1-886913-03-X

Cover illustration: male American Kestrel fledgling with a broken tarsus.

Cover and interior illustrations by Kit Chubb
Cover design by John Luckhurst

Printed in Canada by Friesens

CONTENTS

Acknowledgements   viii

Introduction   1

1   Loons and Grebes   4
    The Loon Landings
    Loon Neck Feathers
    Loon Lucky Twice
    A Water Witch

2   Pelicans   14
    The Pelican Affair

3   The Heron Family   20
    Lost, Strayed, or Abandoned?
    More Eyes That Look Under the Beak
    Introducing "Big Cranky"
    When the Legs Don't Work

4   Ducks and Geese   35
    The Nine Tarbabies
    The Inflatable Merganser
    Of Other Diving Ducks
    The Goose Guest

5   The Story of Yik   44

6   The Hawk Family   55
    An Oar for an Osprey
    Harriers: After the Haybine
    Bill's Way
    The Half-brained Hawk
    About Starvation
    The Hawk That Came Back
    The Story of Left and Right

7 Vultures, Eagles, and Kestrels 76
   The Vulture's Secret Weapon
   Just an Eagle on My Freezer
   Puck
   All Suki's Babies
   An Asphalt Death

8 Moorhens 94
   Semaphore's Secrets

9 Doves and Pigeons 102
   The Peace of the Dove
   The Tale of Bumfeathers
   Feminine Tactics

10 The Owl Family 112
   Romulus
   A Logging Surprise
   Big She
   Bachelor's Baby
   A Box for Wowl
   City Owl
   The Raptor Robber
   A Dreadful Encounter
   Pogo: Defeating the Indefatigable
   A Snowy Flies Home—in a Hercules

11 Woodpeckers 142
   Raising Baby Pileateds

12 Passerines 149
   Games with a Raven

   Epilogue 153

   Glossary 155

   Metric Conversion Table 157

*This book is dedicated to 160 Flying Angels
and to my Robin, husband, partner, and Ark Angel*

ACKNOWLEDGEMENTS

This book was generously assisted by a Canada Council Explorations Grant.

In the confusion of early beginnings, trying to organize and peddle the manuscript myself, I was much helped and heartened by many thoughtful, encouraging letters from editor Lily Poritz Miller. I also thank author and poet Stan Dragland for his vision of "the Ark"; friend and cookbook author Eleanor Thompson, for alternately cheering and consoling me throughout its various fortunes and misfortunes; my children, for sharing *their* bathroom with ducks, loons, and the occasional owl; my husband Robin, without whom the Ark, and the book, would not be.

I also wish to thank my agent, Bella Pomer, who took it on when I gave it up; Jane McHughen at Prairie Books, who agreed to publish it; and my editor, Geri Rowlatt, for her impeccable politeness as she strove to make my breathless sentences more coherent.

Plan of Avian Care and Research Foundation 1987 Including House Plan, Basement Level

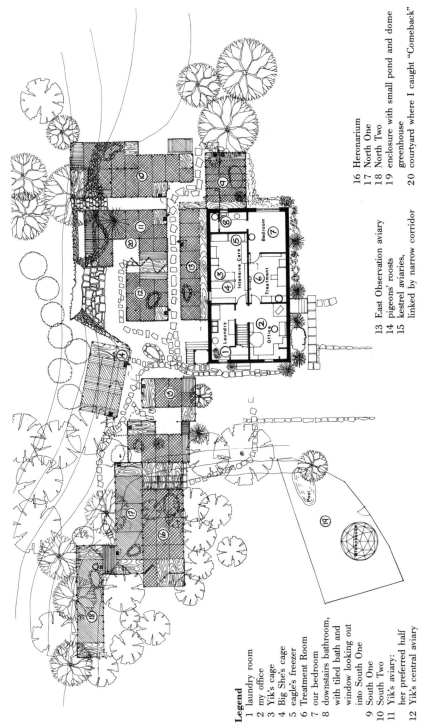

Legend

1 laundry room
2 my office
3 Yik's cage
4 Big She's cage
5 eagle's freezer
6 Treatment Room
7 our bedroom
8 downstairs bathroom,
  with tiled bath and
  window looking out
  into South One
9 South One
10 South Two
11 Yik's aviary:
  her preferred half
12 Yik's central aviary

13 East Observation aviary
14 pigeons roosts
15 kestrel aviaries,
  linked by narrow corridor

16 Heronarium
17 North One
18 North Two
19 enclosure with small pond and dome
  greenhouse
20 courtyard where I caught "Comeback"

THE ROOTS OF THE AVIAN "ARK"

What is This "Ark" and How Did It Come About?

A friend saw it through his poet's eyes as a hospital houseboat at anchor, a wild bird's safe vessel on which damaged passengers rest and heal, despite their evident reluctance to be on board. It seems a fair analogy.

All flora and fauna have always engrossed me. At an early age I unanimously elected myself their lifelong champion, these companionable creatures swimming, hopping, and flying about the ponds and scrubby brush country east of Montreal where I wandered constantly from toddler to teen. One of my father's favorite photographs is of me, aged three, crouching in great delight to touch a large toad. Born in 1936 as an only child of rather old and ailing parents, I was always happiest out-of-doors. I had a bush hideout which served as a blind; I used my allowance to buy and release snakes from local bullies (how often did I pay for the same snake twice?) and started a hospital for stray starvelings in our garden shed, as my parents were rather repressive about wildlife in the house. Even then I did not want to *keep* my captives—I wanted to study and draw them, heal them, and then let them go. My bedroom grew crowded with bugs in boxes, caterpillars in jars, pond life in aquaria, fossils in rocks, shells, skeletons, nests, snakeskin castoffs, and notebooks that grew fat with observations, drawings, and watercolors. My prize acquisition was a lower jaw of a horse. It was my secret life.

When we moved to the wilder countryside in Hudson Heights, Quebec, I at last found a fellow-naturalist, an old fellow who was as obsessed as I, though his passion was fixed to just a single subject:

1

birds. For many years Major Ommanney had been banding the songbirds in his garden, alone, at times alienated (no doubt due to constant warring with the neighbor's cats) till this the last summer of his life when we became instant confederates, happily sharing the incomparable satisfaction of birds in the hand. At last, Achates! A soul-mate! He taught me how to identify, handle, weigh, measure, and even sketch them. I wish he could know how much he influenced me.

My family had no money (and in the fifties, there were no student loans) for the university studies I wanted to take, so drawn by a combination of nursing, biology, and medicine, I became a nurse. The following twelve years of experiences of trauma, treatment, and disease later proved a great advantage as self-taught rehabilitator. I also travelled around Europe on a scooter twice, married twice, and raised six children, which effectively suppressed most wildlife activities.

My preoccupation with natural history resurfaced in 1976 during an introduction to mist-netting, where licenced banders set up two-meter high nets of hair-fine nylon mesh to entangle flying birds, which are quickly removed, recorded, banded, and released. Helen Quilliam, much-loved local author, bird authority, and bander, took me to the banding station at Prince Edward Point one spring. I was so magnetized by birds in hand that I brought my Welsh architect husband Robin down too, and *he* became fascinated, so we promptly became volunteers in the project. We might have stayed that way — as weekend volunteers — but for a small accident.

With my untrained fingers, I unfortunately wrenched some wing muscles of a tiny ovenbird when I was untangling it, and full of remorse, I asked permission to take it home and care for it. This first miniature bird-patient made a powerful impression on me. I spent many hours watching and writing about the shy, delicate little wood warbler as it darted out from its mossy shelter to snatch up minute spiders, sow-bugs, and other delicacies that I had hunted for it. Though its body weighed only six grams, it was a perfect model of nature's vital systems — the same systems and organs we have — all working at high speed. I was filled with questions to which I could find no answers.

The Ark was launched soon after I found my first severely injured bird, desperately needing surgery and expertise far beyond my ability. In vain I searched for an expert. The veterinarians I approached were kindly pet-and-livestock doctors, the government officials were negative, and the only bona fide rehabilitation center was the Owl Rehabilitation and Research Foundation near St. Catharines. So there and then I vowed that we would develop a bird hospital ourselves, and recognizing a mulish glint of obstinacy he had seen before, Robin let himself get hauled into my plans.

First we acquired the government licences to keep wild birds temporarily; then we set in motion the founding of our charitable organization, which in 1978 became the Avian Care and Research Foundation. I got a banding permit, and Robin began designing and constructing well-crafted cages and aviaries. We started breeding mice and mealworms. Donations began to arrive, mostly equipment: an ophthalmoscope; two microscopes; an autoclave; photographic equipment; a set of microdissecting instruments; a pair of precision rongeurs; and best of all, a blessed old dental X-ray machine, to which we added a darkroom, lead accessories, and a viewer. The ability to take immediate radiographs has proved invaluable not only for prompt diagnosis, but also because our continuing studies of bird anatomy and skeletal trauma are almost wholly dependent upon the thousands of X-rays now filed and cross-referenced here.

While Robin and I run the foundation as volunteers without staff, we take this chance to thank several thousand members of the concerned public who provide almost all the funding every year. We are also proud of our "Flying Angels," a band of 160 volunteer "ambulance" drivers on standby call over much of central-eastern Ontario; their unusual service in promptly bringing us the wounded is often lifesaving for the many raptors, herons, and loons they are requested to retrieve. Further, when the bird has recovered, the same Angel often releases it exactly where it was found, an act so essential to the continuity of their interrupted lives.

About the book. It developed informally over the years from my newspaper columns and occasional magazine articles, my case-history notes, and about 130 drawings. Several of the stories are about early patients who made the deepest impressions. Some of the stories are funny, others sad, and a few incredible, but all of them are true. And now at last, you will share them with me.

CHAPTER 1

LOONS AND GREBES

The Loon Landings

On a cold, cloudy morning in mid-December, a fast-travelling loon flew low over a city by a river, braked for a landing, and skidding out of control, belly-flopped to a jolting halt with beaktip slowly dripping blood. Traffic roared by, eight lanes of it, parting and closing around the stranded loon, till a driver boldly stopped and lifted the big body into his car. This was not the river. So why had he landed there?

This Common Loon became our first land-lander. Apart from scraped toes and a missing bit of beaktip, we found no sign of injury, so we did as we were to do for all such subsequent cases: weighed, examined, and X-rayed, taking without rancor our several blows for presuming to lay hands on him. As he rested on his breast on our treatment table, his unsupportive legs splayed flat out on either side, frog-fashion, as the legs of all loons do. Checkup complete, we fastened a numbered international Fish and Wildlife aluminum band on one of his legs and immediately released him into the nearest lake.

A loon *is* water, really, both salt and fresh. Eating, courting, sleeping, preening, and loafing on it, he spends his first three to four years maturing along the ocean's coast before returning to breed on an inland lake—perhaps the lake of his birth. His only time away from water is in the air, on the nest, and during the brief act of copulation. Though the skin of his back is as thin and delicate as that of other waterfowl, on his breast and belly it is thick and tough and protected with dense, wetproofed feathers to keep out water and cushion hard landings. In order to speed along under water in pursuit of arrowswift fish, his powerful legs and feet provide maximal piston-propulsion—and most significantly, the upper two-thirds of those legs are completely contained within the body skin for streamlining. This is what prevents loons from standing upright like a duck on terra firma, and because they cannot stand, they cannot push off to fly, but can only hump along on their breasts. Even on water, their small wings must perform a long hard-beating taxi, as much as half a kilometer (depending on the wind) along the water's surface before their heavy bodies become airborne.

Land-landing loons raise many questions for which we have few answers. Do they mistake rain-silvered macadam for a river? Possibly, for some have been found on wet roads and one landed in a flooded field, but we have had several apparently healthy loons from empty ditches, dirt roads, dry highways, and once, a Toronto skating rink. One even landed in the middle of the Peace Bridge! Could they be temporarily distressed by, say, dizziness, a bad headache, or a cramp? Though documentation of a flying loon being seized with a "charley horse" is lacking, such a possibility may exist: flapping ceaselessly at 260 to 270 wing-beats per minute, those comparatively small wings support up to six kilograms. Could they be weakened by a heavy load of parasites, such as flukes, or environmental pollutants like mercury, DDE, PCBs? Then there is the swallowing of fishhooks or lead sinkers (which cause lead poisoning), being entangled in fishing line or being shot, which are the four routine causes of death in loons we see, but so far none of these four has been implicated in a land-landed loon. And finally, could their choice of landing site occasionally be deliberate? The following case did make us wonder.

This was a Red-throated, the smallest of loons, who, thanks to having a shorter, lighter frame, can actually stagger a few steps and take off with less effort. He made a dramatic entry into the central oval of a small trotting-track a few kilometers from Lake Ontario, where a startled horsewoman picked him up and was shocked to find that, like her horse, he was bridled—but with two rings of a plastic six-pack carrier, the other four rings being firmly jammed over his head. Luckily, he appeared to have been gagged thus for only a few days, for we found his mouth nearly undamaged, and we banded and released him at once. Two questions: Did he intentionally seek a human being? And how did he get his head tangled in the plastic coils? That kind of plastic garbage floats, and from loon behavior here, I'd guess that he investigated it in simple curiosity as it floated by. Discarded plastic six-pack carriers don't look lethal, but they are.

■   ■   ■

Though it was several years ago, the pleasant images of our first earthbound loon's release are fresh in my mind still. After apologizing for shutting him into a travelling box, Robin and I drove to a quiet shore of Verona Lake, where together we opened the box close to the water. After a few impatient awkward breastings over the grating pebbles, the loon reached the edge and floated freely, transformed. Home. Silently he glided to greater depth where he dipped his head in deeply, looking left and right underwater in a professional manner before slipping into a dive and surfacing to shake his wings mightily. Would he make an eerie, wild cry of triumph to express his emotions? We waited tensely, but apparently we were not going to be so honored. But he did make a small expectoration that sounded like "pfui," as he spat out a narrow strip of *Whig-Standard* journalism from the box in which he had been so carefully packed. Then he vanished, leaving only a snip of newspaper and a telltale trail of bubbles rising from his special world.

A Common Loon in breeding plumage — this one has a balance problem

Loon Neck Feathers

Feathers are a wonder of genetic engineering, precisely designed for the right season, the right bird, and even the right spot on the bird. Each one has a special purpose of its own. Unseen, the next feather-to-be, microscopic and predesigned, is ready to erupt into the follicle as the old one moults out. Plumage provides waterproofing, warmth, camouflage, and social signals about age, sex, and intent. Recently, as I finished a postmortem on an adult Common Loon that had been shot during the breeding season, I was regretfully stroking the black, velvety ultrasoft head and neck when I noticed that the scintillating vertically striped neckband (a distinctive above-waterline decoration of both adult sexes) was composed of much stiffer, rougher feathers that strongly resisted being ruffled. This intrigued me, so I began to examine it more closely.

The collar, or neckband, was composed of black-and-white verticals, literally outstanding, for the design was in high relief, the white stripes elevated and the black stripes depressed. I pulled a feather out. Its core was black, while its outer area was white. Further, the vanes were not flatly horizontal from the shaft, but grew upward to form a raised V. So each black stripe was a furrow of hundreds of black shafts lying snugged head on tail, while each white stripe was an arch of snowy outer vanes from adjoining rows, stiffly clasped together.

After the breeding season, the flashing visual signals of the neck-collar, the white-patterned black body, melt away to be replaced with shades of blend-in gray. Now, as the loons move to their winter quarters to feed, sleep, moult, preen, and loaf, young and old look alike. Age and territory are of no consequence upon the sea.

Loon Lucky Twice

Here's the story of a Common Loon's three known encounters with man: injured once, then rescued — twice.

The first good occasion took place in November in bush country half a kilometer from the Ottawa River near Castleford. Two woodsmen, jolting their truck over rough ruts that passed for a logging road, spotted a large dark bird collapsed on the thin snow cover. At first they thought it was dead, but on approach it moved feebly, making them fear it was dying. "If I'd had my gun I'd have killed him so he wouldn't suffer," one told me later. "He was nearly done."

However, having no weapon, they gingerly gathered it in a blanket and laid the bird on the floor of the truck. To their astonishment, after only about five minutes of warming up, the resilient loon began to revive and bump about, speeding the homeward journey with startling vocal tremolos and threatening stabs at nearby human limbs. Thus encouraged, they brought him to us.

Like many of the damaged loons we have received, this one had been shot in the duck-hunting season. Left behind in his first encounter with man the enemy, an X-ray revealed a telltale lead pellet embedded in a fully healed, double wing fracture — both radius and ulna broken at the same site. He had probably been fired upon while swimming on the river, and as loons do not use their wings to propel themselves underwater, he simply folded his broken wing in the natural resting position and went on living his normal life. The flowing waters provided prey, and the constant washing cleaned his wounds. In three weeks those fractures were healed, though crookedly, and despite their irregularity were able to support his weight. We thought him lucky, for in our experience such two-bone fractures rarely function properly unless one at least has been surgically pinned.

Rarely, loons have been known to make short forced "marches" from one body of water to another, shoving themselves along with their strong feet, but according to the woodsmen, this loon could not possibly have humped his way from the river. Not only was there a large tract of dense brush to be traversed, but also a hilly ridge that ran parallel to the river's banks. In support of this we noted that neither his breast nor his soles were worn, and we concluded that, despite the ugliness of his healed fractures, he must have flown to where they found him. But why land there? Inference: His flight had been short of its goal . . . perhaps, after all, because of the wing. Ironically, we would never know how well he could fly except by band return, for loons cannot take off in captivity, and newly released loons soon submerge out of sight.

The loon had eaten so well during those flightless weeks that his body was well larded with migratory fat. During his single afternoon with us he snatched fish meals in the pool, argued vehemently about being X-rayed, humped around the office floor, and gave occasional tremolo alarm calls that shivered our skin into gooseflesh. We wasted no time in the sunny mildness of the following morning before tipping him out of his travelling box on a nearby lakeshore and watching with satisfaction as he slid rapidly down the thin rim of snow on the shore and broke the hazy mirrored surface, showing in every possible way his relief to be free again.

■　　■　　■

That was November 25. By December 7, the lake was cooling rapidly, fringed with a warning ribbon of silvering ice, and he was still there. But how could the loon foretell a fall of 14°C overnight, speeding the stealthily advancing ice to the very center, where it would narrowly miss seizing him in its fast-forming grip? He scrambled free in time, but became instead another kind of prisoner, unable to drink, eat, walk, or fly, exposed to wind, predators, and impending death.

He fought it. Two cottagers watching in distress from their lakeside bungalow saw him try over and over to scrabble or fly, and though he made some progress, he was never far from the center. Walking out to him that day was simply too dangerous. Pushing an unwieldy aluminum boat over the ice proved impossible. How, then? They phoned us. Since unusual measures seemed called for, I suggested that they try Kingston's CKWS TV to see if a short broadcast would bring help. Their call never got past the newsroom for the news director, a loon-lover, took up the challenge to try to find a magic solution and by heaven, he did, though arrangements would not be complete until the following day. His triumph: he had persuaded the owner of a Hovercraft to pilot his machine over the lake, had borrowed a wide trailer for its transport, and had organized a TV video crew to record the rescue. Mutual compassion had now linked eleven strangers together. The twelfth was yet to come.

While all these technicalities were being coordinated, Robin and I ran around trying to give morning care to the patients, to answer the phone, and to find our skis and woollies. Though we had never seen a Hovercraft in action, we thought that it might frighten the loon shoreward to safer ice on which we could ski. This too was all part of a grand scheme that was never to take place after all.

With a countdown of just nine minutes before the Hovercraft was to begin its journey to the lake, a slim local young countryman, who had earlier been phoned by the frantic cottager, quietly arrived at the opposite side of the lake armed with only a small canoe, a "spud" (long-handled ice-fishing axe) and a cardboard box. Pushing the canoe alongside, he walked steadily out, testing the creaking, glassy ice ahead with the spud. Shouted warnings from the cottager did not deter Keith Harper as he advanced on the loon, who, after a frantic leap in the air that actually led to about thirty meters of flight, now lay nearly spent. Keith circled him cautiously before putting the carton beside him, whereupon the loon gave a last mighty leap and flipped right into the box! Now with loon in box and box in canoe, Keith walked calmly back to shore. He was shyly surprised by the warmth of his reception afterward; to him it was simply a natural response to a winter's challenge on a lake, a subject with which he was quite familiar—he had been raised on the adjoining one.

When we checked the loon over thoroughly we found that though he was thirsty and his feet were scraped, he was only one hundred grams less than two weeks before; in our bathtub he rectified this deficiency by gulping a large whitefish—on TV, for by now the camera crew had caught up with us. (Imagine the bedlam in our bathroom!) Always aware of how fast a loon can lose vital waterproofing, we asked if, on their return to Kingston, the crew would release it in Lake Ontario (parts of which remain open all winter) and this they did.

Would this loon be able to fly the hundreds of kilometers to winter with his fellow loons? We'll probably never know, for band recoveries are few, while guns, fishhooks, monofilament line, lead sinkers, acid rain, and ocean pollution threaten loons everywhere. But thanks to everyone who had joined our venture, this one at least had been given a chance—a lucky second time.

A Water Witch

If I have a choice of which bird I shall be in the Next Life, please! I'd like to be a grebe.

The arrival of our first toylike charmer decided me at once. Like the loon, he had been found squatting on the December marsh ice, and to judge by his excessive weight loss, he had been dry and empty for some days. Unlike the loon, he fitted neatly in the palm of my hand, watching me with the most remarkable eyes: vivid scarlet irises spangled with a ring of golden dots around pinpoint pupils. Restlessly, he paddled the air with his strange diver's feet—toes not webbed together but flatly lobed, looking like three brown leaves and a leaflet. He could even run a short distance on them. As I longed to study those little propellors underwater, I filled the biggest aquarium we had, rigged floodlights and a camera on a tripod, and popped the little fellow in.

It's hard to know who was more stimulated, he or I. The dried-out little Horned Grebe ecstatically rolled, dived, and burst up through the surface flapping so madly that the hot floodlights hissed with splatter. While Robin drove off to buy a bucket of minnows from the nearest bait shop, I dropped in live mealworms (beetle larva we breed for woodpeckers) which the grebe snapped up hungrily as they sank; but it was the introduction of the live fish that showed us his otterlike agility. Even in the confines of the aquarium, his grace and speed were breathtaking as he zoomed in twisting pursuit. In less than three minutes he had swallowed twenty, his full crop now a-shimmy with the bulges of neatly packed fish—the last ones still squirming!

Grebes, who spend their frenetic lives in, on, and under water, are endowed with an unusual ability. They can sink slowly and unobtrusively below the surface till they just disappear, and make off so sinuously and rapidly that they were long ago dubbed "hell-diver" and "water witch"; the latter probably because when they dive or sink they seem to stay under forever, though they are soon secretly assessing the danger from the nearest vegetation, with just their nose and scarlet eyes playing periscope.

I knelt at the camera, clicking away in absorption till suddenly his other major problem became shockingly apparent: no waterproofing. Now resting at the surface, his body was slowly sinking below the waterline and his head and neck feathers were spikily soaked to the skin, sending him into a shivering fit. I hurriedly scooped him out into a towel, squeezed him till the pile was soggy, and set him to dry under a brooder

A hell-diver with no waterproofing

lamp; ah, with his plumage plastered so flat that skin peeped through, he was a puny thing. Under the heat he immediately began vigorously setting his coat to rights till at last he rested, finally dry, a second creature altogether—lighter, softer, silkier, his singularity confirmed by those compelling carmen eyes.

Waterproofed plumage is a natural asset of healthy birds, not for convenience, but for survival. Every bird's familiar frequent preening is mainly to perfect and renew his waterproofing. Concealed among the feathers on his rump is a small bulbous gland with a wick, the uropygial gland. This he pinches, first wiping some of the oily secretion on his back where he can rub the top of his head in it, and then rapidly spreading more to the rest of his feathers as he whips each one through his beak. The greatest stimulus for preening is being wet. Full waterproofing is indispensable for such diving birds as loons and grebes, for if water can penetrate through the dense air-filled down-feathers to the skin they become greatly chilled. To compensate they begin to stay out of the water, which rapidly increases the loss of waterproofing, which in turn increases the time spent out of the water, till no protection remains at all. I think that the natural cycle is more complex still, and when interrupted by illness or trauma, waterproofing is difficult (occasionally impossible) to restore till the next moult.

It took our fearless little grebe ten days to regain his waterproofing. We supplied him with a "shoreboard in the sun" and left on his own, he established his own wash cycle. Following a brief minute-long spin he would clamber out to digest, warm, and preen till dry; then Plop! back for another minute of whirling agitation in the aquarium (which we emptied and refilled four times every day), then chase, gobble, and scramble out again, soaked and bulgy-busted. As he gained in strength and liveliness he stabbed ferociously at all unwary fingers; the aquarium began to leak; he ate up a whole baitshop and started on another; I ran out of towels; and just when we were beginning to wonder if the whole thing was a loop, he suddenly became totally waterproofed. What a difference! Now he rarely went ashore, and even after the most lengthy and arduous of aquabatics he shot to the surface dry and powderpuffy, and took to sleeping on the water overnight as healthy grebes do. His weight had jumped to normal . . . he was ready to go back to the wild.

Two days later Jean-Louis Frund, a well-known French-Canadian nature filmmaker and supporter of ours, joined us at the Cataraqui River just above the locks, where the river opens widely for half a kilometer or more—an ideal release spot. Under the stern eye of the director's camera we obediently banded the grebe and introduced him into the shallows of the river where even at this time of year, small fish could be seen darting by. He saw them too, and made a number of frisky dives.

Presently, as if curious, he swam back toward us and called several times, though he had never voiced a note till then. Under the circumstances, they were sweet sounds to hear.

CHAPTER 2

PELICANS

The Pelican Affair

A wonderful bird is the pelican,
His bill will hold more than his belican.
He can take in his beak
Food enough for a week,
But I'm damned if I see how the helican.

Dixon Lanier Merritt, 1910

We get so many phone calls about wildly misidentified birds in trouble that we seldom ask for details anymore. "An owl with big eyes" may be an owl, or may be a kestrel, and once it was a whip-poor-will; while "a hawk with a hooked beak" may be a hawk, or may be a grouse, and once it was a battery chicken. It depends. So some skepticism may have been warranted here:

Lady Caller: "We just picked up a pelican on the 401. Can we bring it to you right away?"

Me: "A pelican, eh?" (rolling my eyes about for the amusement of my listening family). "Good for you. By all means bring it — see you soon." To Robin: "Sounds like another Herring Gull on the way," and we giggled together over the avian ignorance of the public.

Presently, the door opened and two attractive ladies descended our stairs to the treatment room, the foremost awkwardly carrying a huge white . . . pelican. I was stunned. This species was not only on the "Threatened" list in both Canada and the United States at that time, but it was even classed as "Endangered" in Ontario, the

14

only colonies being on the western border of the province. My mind was shocked right out of gear, and the leading lady laughed out loud at the expression on my face.

The pelican, released from her perfumy embrace, stood solidly on his large orange feet and assessed us with fearless curiosity before climbing solemnly onto the bathroom scales hurriedly put before him and beginning a busy all-body preen while we four simply sat around him on the rug and stared. He was too absorbed to notice. Presently he stopped and suddenly everted his pouch in a huge inside-out rubbery stretch over his neatly coiled neck in a gargantuan yawn, or was it a moué of distaste? Perhaps the former, for he then buried his long beak straight down his back under a spray of feathers and went to sleep, though one dark Cyclops eye kept "obbo" on us for a while.

He climbed on the scales hurriedly placed before him

As he had been found on the Trans-Canada, he had either hit high-power wires overhead or had been struck by a vehicle, for he had a broken wing. By the greatest good luck he was wearing a Fish and Wildlife band proving he had been banded as a chick in Minnesota that June, about five months previously. Having been blown about fifteen hundred kilometers in the wrong direction by strong October winds, it was little wonder he was tired out and weighed only five kilograms, which seemed insufficient for his huge bulk. A dead fish was offered for his inspection and found wanting, so impatiently I opened his beak and popped it in, trying hard to keep his head up as he struggled vainly to eject it. I won, but I never expected to meet a bird that could evert his beak and turn his head completely upside down at the same time! I hoped he would feed himself soon before he was strong enough to give me a real argument. But now I decided it was his bedtime, so I carefully picked him up in my arms—a pleasant sensation of gigantic kapok-filled cushion, warm and trusting. His skin felt baggy and his feathers gave off crackly impressions as if he were indeed lined with plastic. I set him down on a big pile of soft pine needles in the corner of the laundry room for the night, where he promptly lay flat on his belly to sleep.

Next morning he hid shyly behind the water-heater, still too exhausted to eat, though he considered it. He toyed with fish in water, in my hand, and on the pine needles, even taking a small one into his incredible stretchy pouch and flipping it rhythmically up and down like a bored short-order cook playing with a pancake, but the only fish he actually swallowed were shoved in there by me. We X-rayed his broken metacarpal bone, for which he only needed a lightweight thermoplastic cast which took about twenty seconds to apply, and once on, he hardly noticed, for it was designed not to hamper his movements; he could stretch all of the big wing except the wrist supported by the cast.

Perhaps it was as well he was slightly limited. A White Pelican's wingspan is the largest of northern birds, and there was hardly room indoors for the strongly swinging wing-and-a-half as he later stood on his stump and exercised every day. The wind of it whirled things about and showed the shining perfection of the wing's lovely shape, unexpectedly displaying the black primary feathers that are hidden at rest.

But today was all jet lag. After several more naps (usually lying down, often with that one disconcerting eye watching the traffic go by), I carried him into our bath for the treat of a warm shower to maintain his waterproofing, but to my surprise he gave no sign of enjoying it, nearly falling sleep again instead. Bath over, I wrapped him in a big beach towel and carried him tenderly back to his clean peli-pad where he set about preening industriously—a percussive rapid tapping with the hard end of his beak, which became a routine tattoo audible three rooms away, even in the middle of the night. (It was the only sound he ever made, except loud digestive rumblings when he was hungry.) Wings, back, tummy, tail . . . How did he ever manage the short, velvety feathers of his long neck, I wondered, but perhaps the gray upper three-quarters were only washed and drip-dried by the rains of nature. Perhaps all these creatures look as if they have collar-grime; after all, he was the first I had seen.

A pelican's beak is an extraordinary organ. His long upper structure was gently flexible, warm, shiny-smooth pink, and tipped with a gleaming orange "claw." The thin, flattened nostrils were hard to find, though on a few later occasions they dripped "tears" when his revived appetite was about to be sated. On the lower mandible, which was also pink and extremely flexible, was this perma-pleated orange crepe pouch so different in texture that it might have been an afterthought sewn onto his neck. When he gaped widely, I could see a protective fleshy tube surrounding the glottis; I never got a good look at this thing because he objected to my attempts at dental scrutiny, but I suppose its purpose was to keep water from getting into his lungs while scooping up his fish dinners. He could stretch that pouch to an incredible width, as he demonstrated whenever one of his admirers tossed him a fish, fielding it as fast and as neatly as a boy with an expanding catcher's mitt.

Our delightful pelican was with us nearly two weeks. Soon he stopped peeking modestly around the heater and took over the whole laundry room, which we hurriedly carpeted in astroturf and covered with clear vinyl to protect his delicate soles from the cold hardness of the concrete floor. Daily he grew stronger and heavier, for when I peered between his thickset legs as he toed-in on the bathroom scale, I saw a gain from five to six kilograms. Certainly his daily intake grew bigger, from eight hundred grams of perch, rock bass, and crappie to over sixteen hundred grams, all of which he pincered up dextrously from hand or bucket, juggled into the correct position by feel, and tossed uphill to the summit of his throat before swallowing them rapidly down. The first meal of the day might total seven hundred grams.

The pelican gave me a dreadful fright on his sixth day by having an early-morning body-shaking fit of what appeared to be uncontrollable panting. Oh, God, alkalosis, I thought, and tore around giving him antibiotics and Ringer's Lactate solution with Vitamin B by tube down his throat, which he thoroughly resented, managing to return at least a third of each dose into my shoes. He was a great responsibility to me and I worried miserably all day, phoning experts, hovering anxiously over our precious charge as much as I could.

It was difficult, though, for the media was after our precious charge too, and there was no rest from journalists, photographers, and phone calls. As it turned out, close observation showed that nearly every morning after his first, large, freshly thawed and chilly breakfast, the pelican had a similar shivering session and he had never been ill at all!

The most amazing thing about him was his playful behavior with us, for while birds do play in the wild, they do not do so with their keepers in captivity. He was, however, a young colonial member suddenly separated from the comforting crowd and he was probably bored as well as lonely. Accordingly, although he was confined to the laundry room by a low fence in the doorway, he stationed himself close by, often even sleeping nights there, in order not to miss any entertainment that might be going on. Whenever I was in the laundry room kneeling to wash the plastic rug-protector (which was very often—this bird squirted a big puddle of recycled fish every nine to twelve minutes), he followed me about wanting to play with me, grabbing at the sponge, my rubber gloves, my clothes, and even my hair. Stolen items were "chewed," tossed in the air, and fetched back again. If nothing else was available, even unwanted fish corpses were bounced about, till he grew weary of the game and then hid them somewhere. Newspapers were snatched and flung about with zest; human hands were responsive when chewed on, toes were always amusing, and he goosed me twice. The first time was early on in his stay and I was taken by surprise while bending over the laundry sink; my gluteus maximus was caressed as by an expert hand and then pinched hard. The second time occurred during a national TV news filming, but thankfully they censored it.

Winter in Canada is no place for a pelican, and in order to transfer him south, I called up Monte Hummel. Monte is the dynamic Executive Director of the Canadian branch of the World Wildlife Fund, an international organization concerned with endangered animals. Monte not only arranged the government transit permits, the admission to a Florida rehabilitation center, the flight bookings from Toronto to Miami to Tampa, Florida, but also saw to it that the WWF paid our costs. Finally, he drove the six-hundred-kilometer round trip from Toronto with his friend Dan to pick up the pelican and put it on the plane himself, bringing the biggest molded-vinyl dog carrier that Air Canada could provide.

That evening our farewell celebrations turned into a pelican party.

Dan did stand-up comic turns that made us howl with laughter, Monte told rousing tales of his adventures, Robin and I passed out refreshments, and we all played with the pelican, who became very invigorated with all the attention and cavorted lightheartedly with us all. When it was time for him to enter his temporary home, he waddled ahead of me readily enough till he reached the cage door where he abruptly put on his brakes, so I gave him a rude shove from behind (it was my turn!) and closed the door. By his nonplussed expression, he considered it a barbarous thing to do to an unsuspecting friend.

He was released later that spring into a large and noisy Florida colony of fellow pelicans, so I do hope he has forgotten all about it.

CHAPTER 3

THE HERON FAMILY

Lost, Strayed, or Abandoned?

The farmer reached inside his jacket and withdrew a bundle of wiggling ginger down which he set casually on my desk. Its long legs were polished jade, its bill a patterned spear. The baby American Bittern showed no fear as he stood planted sturdily on outsized green feet, bright eyes watching us expectantly, while I'm afraid to say we all just gaped in astonishment. Just as I noticed that one wing was dangling awkwardly, the fuzzy chick gave a sudden mewing hunger-cry that galvanized us into action; Robin hurried to get some lean beef (it was in our first year, before we had any mice) while I began to make a support for the wing. At this point the farmer withdrew reluctantly, saying yet again how glad he was to finally find someone who would take care of the hungry wanderer he had found unexpectedly among his hens, one of which was probably the perpetrator of the fracture.

We wondered why the baby had strayed into a henyard instead of being under the guidance of a parent bittern, and then we learned that domestic fowl might attract a bittern chick because the clucky lingo sounds somewhat familiar. (Later we learned from our banding of bittern chicks that after leaving the nest they do not stay under the guidance of a parent, but wander alone as much a kilometer a day, eating, growing, and experiencing life: from then on, we simply put them back.)

Like some other of our new arrivals who had not yet learned fear, his peaceful compliance allowed us to support his greenstick fracture of the humerus without any fuss; in such a young bird it only needed a lightweight splint, if anything, for it was in good alignment. He then ate voraciously of beef strips and grasshoppers, gave himself a quick lick, and abruptly fell asleep under the warmth of the desk lamp.

The following morning proved to be another sunny June pleasure, so we took the little creature down to our four-meter-diameter geodesic dome greenhouse in which he could start his new life. The sandy floor was circled with raised beds forested with vigorous climbing tomatoes and overgrown lettuce which the baby bittern seemed to find quite to his liking, for he at once disappeared into the sheltering greenery.

American Bittern chick with an unnecessary splint

He had barely settled in when the farmer phoned again, very excited. "You'll never believe this," he exclaimed. "I've found *another* one with the hens!" So not long afterwards we all trooped down to the greenhouse again, this time to introduce the second, slightly older chick—uninjured, a lot more hungry but a lot less friendly than the first. After a mighty meal snatched with dark suspicion from our fingers, the elder was beginning to explore the greenhouse vegetation when the younger bittern appeared suddenly. The elder struck out instinctively, but a second later came recognition—they relaxed, brushed up against each other, in a warmly familiar way, and with one accord turned their backs on us, and stalked off together into the bush. Thus united and comforted, the little orphans set about making the strange heavy-scented tomato plants their quarters, and thereafter they always slept curled up in a snug saffron heap and spent most of their daytime meanderings in each other's company.

After a few days they found that the greenhouse door opened invitingly into a large marshy enclosure containing a small pond carefully prepared for them. In the shallow end I had corralled its live inhabitants with an underwater screen, and on the bank I had built a reed lean-to for shade, though the bitterns came to spend as much time on top of the roof as under it. At first sight of water and its denizens, they began to stalk small live wigglies at once in an unexpectedly professional manner. Soon we were obliged to go "fishing" for them in local streams every day, returning sweaty and mud-spattered with buckets of large polliwogs, crayfish, beetles, shiners, and whatever else we could dredge up for their ever-increasing appetites.

Before and after eating, the bitterns showed us a charming but rather unbirdlike facet of themselves. They licked their lips . . . or rather, they licked their lower mandible. Just the sight of a minnow would cause the long slender tongue to extrude itself limply over the edge in a slow caress, first whetting one side of the beak and then the other, and thus they daintily polished up after a meal as well. It was an amusing sight, for in the absence of other body signals, the tongue seemed to have a mind of its own. When the beak was holding fresh-caught prey, it too went through a deliberate ritual; a grasshopper, for instance (which all creatures consider a great treat), would be subjected to much careful revolving, rotating, and positioning before it would finally be swallowed head first.

As the bitterns matured, the difference in their personalities became more accentuated each day. The younger, seeing one of us step over the stile with sloshing dinner bucket in hand, would hurry forward, whickering eagerly, mouthing our hands impatiently, or snatching fish straight from the container. In contrast, the elder would have retreated deep into the tall reeds, rewarding our efforts to offer food with defensive posturing — a hissing, wide-mouthed crouch with raised, outfanned head feathers parted dead center. If further antagonized, he would spread his wings to inflate his size still more, and when cornered, he struck the offender painfully. Though he fished in our absence, his supplementary beef rations had to be hurled at his feet, and evening roundup (to return them to the safety of the greenhouse, out of reach of cats, raccoons, and owls) was not without its problems.

One day I came upon the two squatting close together, immobile, with their bills and necks pointed rigidly skyward, and neither made the slightest acknowledgement of my approach. What potential enemy had transfixed them? I craned my neck up too, squinting, but the soaring hawk was so high that it was only a speck to me. How far they could see! Yet they themselves could not be seen from any angle, their long beaks and lengthwise brown stripes blending perfectly with reeds or rushes.

They were growing so fast that a disaster almost befell the younger chick, for on the sixth day I found his healing wing horribly green and swollen with fluid. I rushed to cut the tape off the splint, which he had literally outgrown and which was now cutting off his circulation instead. Luckily I was in time, and the swelling flowed away without problems. The humerus was now callused and needed no further help (if that was what it was) from me.

By now the unfolding real feathers from the stubble of their quills had transformed their appearance, though when backlighted, their endearing ginger baby-down haloed heads and bodies still. The elder began to exercise his wings, developing a peculiar leap-and-flap-madly routine that looked very determined but didn't get him much off the ground (luckily, as their fence was only one-and-a-half meters high and without roof). Soon the younger followed suit, kangarooing about in bursts of comic exuberance, and waving his newly sprouting primaries like flags. But one of these days their wings would carry them off, and then what? The small nearby marsh was now drought-struck, so we observed their progress with mixed pride and anxiety.

When twenty-three days had passed, making them just over four weeks old, the elder tensed, leaped, and sprang into an exhilarating and graceful maiden flight to the end of the enclosure. That was the signal we had been watching for. Early next morning we fed them generously, put them in large toilet-paper cartons stamped in large letters "Pink" and "Yellow," and loaded up bitterns, canoe, cameras, and related impedimenta for the drive to a peaceful, shallow lake lined with cattails and alive with small frogs. The cartons quivered on the bottom of the canoe while we paddled quietly down the lake, and though Pink sneezed and Yellow hissed, the voyage was accomplished without mishap.

When we found a suitable spot, we disembarked, and with the camera ready and a box in front of each of us, we counted "One, Two, Three, GO!" and opened the cartons simultaneously. The elder, apparently shot from a catapult, became an indistinguishable blur on the film, hissing and grawking into infinity. Meantime the younger, as fearless and relaxed as ever, hadn't even completed climbing out of his box on which he then perched languidly as he gazed about his new surroundings while the deerflies buzzed maddeningly about our heads. We gently tipped the container to speed him up, and on land at last, he slowly began to explore the reed-forest.

Retreating to the canoe, we felt that odd mixture of pleasure, relief, and sadness known to most of us as the train or plane carrying away a friend starts its journey. As we pushed off, I managed to snatch up a small frog, and we glided over to present our last offering. The bittern had picked his leisurely way out to a little headland now and stood watching the world at the edge of the cattails, exposed and yet so camouflaged that he appeared and disappeared in our sight by the mere act of a blink. Splat! As the frog hit the water in front of him, instincts of thousands of years suffused his form as slowly, slowly, he stalked that frog, his neck swaying from side to side as he gathered himself for the strike. Out shot his beak and there was small surprised froggie by the leg, being juggled with exaggerated care into exactly the right position for dinner.

We paddled off, singing, our last impression of the friendly bittern being his long tongue gliding pleasurably over the sides of his beak, savoring the gourmet treat.

More Eyes That Look Under the Beak

There's a Lilliputian heron that stands just taller than your coffee mug and weighs the same as a robin; a rare bird, uncommonly heard and seldom seen. Only about every two years do we have the delight of one of these Least Bitterns in the hand, usually because they have been injured flying low to cross a road from marsh to marsh. When one has been examined and set down on the treatment table, he neither flies to escape nor rushes to hide but plants himself—bill high, eyes fixed on us round the sides of his bill—rocking his neck back and forth to the wind-blown sway of invisible reeds. If one of us, irresistibly drawn to touch him, gently advances a finger, Smack!

he stabs it stoutly with his darning-needle beak. Though each seems so insubstantial, I have watched one eat his weight in minnows in a day. My fascination with the Least is not just that he is small, but that he is a miniature — as if one had painted a Great Blue Heron with bold strokes of rust, ocher, and black and then looked at him through the wrong end of a telescope.

Early one evening in May, two birding Angels of ours brought us a male Least they had found on a causeway leading to Presqu'ile Provincial Park. Bruised and bleeding from the cloaca, scraped on the legs, tail pulled out, he had been concussed, probably by being bounced off the bottom of a passing car, its tire briefly gripping his tail feathers. The loss of his stubby tail was an inconvenience, no more, and would be quickly replaced; for in small birds these loosely set feathers function as a safety feature designed to come out easily if snatched by a predator. Soon after his arrival the Least's bleeding stopped, and though shocked and shaken, he could now fly, grip, and walk. The most important sign we found when we examined him was a seasonal bareness on his belly — a brood-patch — indicating that he had recently been sharing the incubation of eggs with his mate and making it imperative that he be returned at once. As it was now after dark with still a long drive to Presqu'ile, a compromise was reached. Our Angels drove him back, and the now-banded tiny bittern slept in a box overnight and was released at the causeway the following dawn. When they opened the box, the Least flew up and out in a wide circle; but before the circle was complete, there were *two* Leasts flying together, heading purposefully into the marsh like one bird.

■　　■　　■

Another uncommon member of this family is the Black-crowned Night Heron, a pale chunky bird with rather short legs and astonishing large scarlet eyes, who also makes use of stillness for camouflage and defense. We have only had one, who had left half a wing in a leghold trap set in shallow water for a muskrat but which often catches herons, owls, and ducks as well. We gave him euthanasia, for we consider it barbaric to keep one-winged or one-legged prisoners except where the breeding of a rare species is a possibility.

Though not classed yet as "rare," there are few enough of these delightful Night Herons that their colonies are monitored by the Canadian Wildlife Service, and one spring I tagged along to help band the young on Pigeon Island in Lake Ontario. Actually I spent a lot of the allotted time taking photographs instead, for being in a breeding colony is an unforgettable experience. The untidy stick nests, built about head height in a tangled barrier of scrubby wild lilacs, were overflowing with scrawny, screaming chicks that bared their back teeth, figuratively speaking, to demonstrate with violent regurgitation their rejection of our interference. A shower of decomposing but entirely recognizable fish fillets, scales, and guts flung out on a sweaty, well-scratched bander was indeed a powerful rebuff.

Six years later I heard that those same lilacs had finally withered and collapsed under their annual burden of concentrated nitrates and the little colony had relocated itself on another island.

Introducing "Big Cranky"

Seated stiffly on a stool in a dark shed, I spy through a window into a spacious sunlit aviary dotted with trees and bushes, my entire attention on its single occupant, a Great Blue Heron. Long of leg, neck, and beak, he preens in blissful privacy. My seat creaks, causing him to freeze and fix me with a long suspicious stare of such directness it is hard to believe he cannot see me at all; but it is impossible, for it is a one-way window. Is something there? Very slowly he approaches till we are face to face, the soft curves of his expressive neck now ramrod stiff, his bulging yellow eyes giving a comical binocular stare under the white chin. He is now taller than I, and from this view his great bicolored beak, sharp in stab and strong in grip, appears reduced, innocuous. I too stay ramrod stiff, for while he is fearful I cannot observe his natural behavior.

Finally after an interminable period of inspection, he at last is satisfied that the

Suspicion

danger has passed, and relaxing his neck once more into the flexible aesthetic curves I love, he swings away, long black toes lifting high and curling carefully after every silent step, managing smoothly considering his tarsus is broken and splinted, the result of an encounter with a Conibear trap. Now his attention has been diverted by a shiver of minnows in the pool and he is again tense, but this time in the pursuit of prey. He lowers and slowly stretches out his neck to nearly horizontal over the surface, suspending it without a tremor for such an endless interval that my own neck aches for him till like a blur he suddenly strikes. With the struggling fish clamped in his beak, he straightens to his full height to swallow it, setting off animated Adam's-apple ripples up and down his neck.

Even with his neck at its straightest, there is a permanent crook created by two of its long vertebrae being set at right angles to each other. Why? Perhaps the kink supports his sleeping posture when his neck is apparently curled into a half-hitch with his beak hidden down his back; or perhaps it is an engineering device to brace that long neck for those periods of immobility, followed by that flashing lunge so remarkable to see.

■　　■　　■

Of all the regular clientele of rehabilitators I know, the Great Blue Heron is considered one of the least wanted and most troublesome. Little wonder, for they are exacting to nourish, demanding to house, and difficult to handle, making the rural American nickname "Big Cranky" rather appropriate in captivity. Unlike other workers, however, I have always been strongly drawn to them—an affinity stirred by their vulnerability and fragility, I think, as well as their elegance of proportion. We have had hundreds of them now, but every problem we have surmounted, every heron we have released, has been a hard-won accomplishment.

These varied problems aside, I suspect that their release rates will always remain lower than those of most of the common admissions, for two reasons. First, despite their size, they are incredibly fragile, both physically and psychologically; second, they are so wild and wary that they are often not caught after an injury—frequently a badly smashed humerus—until it is solidly callused into an impossible shape, or horribly infected and seething with maggots, or the poor heron is simply dying of starvation. By our records about one-third of new arrivals are critically starved after trauma and proceed to die no matter what is done for them. At least another third will have to have euthanasia for the hopelessness of their injuries.

Another reason I champion Big Cranky is that his entire species seems so precarious for the future. Like prehistoric dinosaurs, their big bodies are governed by small brains—the two six-gram eyes flank an eight-gram brain, or about 1/250 of the body weight. (Man's brain is about 1/50 of his body weight.) Such an instinctive brain is less adaptable to such environmental changes as dead lakes, loss of marshlands, reduction of privacy, and the continuous removal of mature stands of trees required for nesting colonies. Further, it has been demonstrated with what appalling ease a whole heronry (up to 350 nests) kronking with lively chicks can be wiped out in a single day when human disruption panics the parents away en masse, leaving the babies to chill, overheat, starve, or be preyed on in their absence.

Great Blue Herons are loyal to their particular heronry. During the once-a-year breeding season, the herons return to the same stand of tall trees to raise their spindly youngsters, who are aloft on their nest for two whole months, eating enormously. As each parent lands neatly on its bulky swaying platform of sticks (how *do* the babies stay aboard?), he or she is urgently solicited to regurgitate a slither of fresh-caught prey onto the floor of the nest where it is eagerly snatched up and reswallowed by the hungry youngsters. (It is worth noting that species who feed their young by this method of reversed peristalsis can, in response to quite a different stimulus, induce the mechanism with ease.) The main items are frogs and fish, but all the heron family are sharp-eyed opportunists that will seize any unwary thing that passes by including snakes, mice, rats, shrews, birds, insects, and crustaceans. Curiously, as in loons, the crayfish legs I find on postmortem are always a bright reddish orange, "cooked" in stomach acid.

By midsummer the youngsters are nearly full-sized, standing and flapping restlessly on their small island in the sky, and soon our heron season at the Ark begins. Admissions of these immatures outnumber adults 5:1 as the unfortunate novices get into trouble. They collide with cars and overhead wires, get shot and caught in leghold traps, swallow fish-with-hook and strangle on the line, fall into oily pools, or are found starving for reasons unknown. One died from swallowing a smooth branch he probably mistook for a fish in the dark; another choked to death on an immature muskrat he was unable to get either down or back. About the only common misfortune they have avoided so far is hitting windows, but I feel confident that this last blunder is one, at least, that the Great Blue Heron is unlikely to add to his repertoire.

Despite many years of working with my beloved giraffe-birds, their care remains more time consuming, costly, and disheartening than that of other species, partly because they suffer such fear. When they must be captured for treatment, being cornered brings on desperate efforts to drive off the enemy with formidable beak-stabbing accompanied by dreadful hollow groans when caught. These trumpeting blasts of unnerving despair vibrate through the lanky body you try to grip, accompanied by an occasional flailing whack from a large wing or the strange cold clutch of a pedalling foot. Most of his stress can be reduced by approaching with a large towel in front which is dropped over the heron's head, causing him to then collapse into a reasonably cooperative heap till he gets a peek out, and then he's a flurry of long limbs again.

Sometimes a slow approach to a standing immature heron, particularly if one stoops to reduce the threat, brings on a "beaksnap." The bird blows up his neck with air and snakes his bill toward you, clapping it suddenly just inches from your nose. Snap! I have been the object of this defensive gesture many times and am convinced that though the heron could easily make a hole in my head, physical contact is not intended, but it always makes me flinch just the same.

Then there is the critical problem of getting them—and keeping them—nourished. These birds are "grazers," catching and eating small prey at irregular intervals all day long, so there must be a whole day's supply of food available from which to choose when desired. Though I sometimes offer laboratory mice and rats, I find fish the best regular fare, which outdoors in winter here means providing heating-cables under their buckets. Before they can even begin, however, they need something live to trigger the first act of feeding: a minnow swimming in a bucket will do. This is followed by dead fish in the same bucket—they average seven hundred grams of fish every day, or about 38 percent of the average heron's body weight. We buy, weigh, package, and freeze such preferred items as perch and sunfish and herring—O loathsome smell!—which they will accept, provided they are left entirely undisturbed. They are terrified by man, the sight of him, the advance of him, probably even the thought of him: an approaching person as far away as twelve meters may represent their critical distance. Just opening their aviary door or even giving a long look can cause the captive heron to bend over and throw up his entire stomachful; any further stress may prevent him from eating again for hours, or even until the next day.

If the heron manages to eat after all that, it is presupposed that he can stand upright on his own two feet (or one foot and a cast) in order to straighten his neck for gravity-assisted swallowing. Though I did once see a prone heron pick up and swallow a small mouse, they usually either cannot or will not eat lying down, and if you help, as fast as you push a fish down he will usually return it, even though the fish is now travelling backward against its spines. If one leg cannot bear weight and the heron can neither rise nor walk, he soon loses heart.

Another concern is the matter of space for walking and shelters for hiding. Indoors, each needs a private room to himself. While we now provide this in our new clinic, for the first twelve years we could only offer the pelican's open laundry room where refuge was the hot-water heater reinforced by a screen, behind which each heron would thankfully retire from view. When restlessness seized him in the quiet of the night, he occasionally took advantage of the freedom to take a little nocturnal ramble, and more than once a soft rustling in our bedroom woke us to see a dim shadow walking slowly past the end of our bed. Though we lay quietly, when he knew that we knew, he turned quietly about and quickened his pace for "home."

■   ■   ■

While convalescing outdoors, each heron needs a large aviary that provides open space to walk, trees with suitable perches, a pool from which to fish, and shelters in which to hide. When we had all of this (including the one-way window) in the newly built "heronarium," though it seemed a haven for one heron, we found it could be confining for two or more. In fact the immatures, who seemed unlikely to develop territorial opinions, seemed downright intolerant of having newer prisoners added to their confines—Heaven knows what adults might have done. One of the main problems was caused by their driving need to pace; invariably each heron saw in his little mind only one possible pacepath . . . the same one, single-laned at that, always along the side of the heronarium furthest from our house. This resulted in two herons restlessly racewalking back and forth, confronting each other once a trip, and stopping to trumpet, strike, and crest like bottlebrushes. Though it looked and sounded fearful, I did not interfere, for careful observation showed that, like the beak-snapping gestures of the indoor herons, the blows never connected.

.   ∎   ∎

It must be a matter of personality. Sometimes when I was obliged to put three Great Blues together in that same cramped space, they surprised me by settling down quite amiably after the completion of introductory formalities. But one crowded August when the aviary already held two immatures, a large and a small — call them male and female — and I added a large third — call him a male — I recorded a most unexpected response. I should add that two subadult bitterns were also convalescing in the aviary at the time.

There was the expected reconnaissance, avoidance, and introductory grawking on approach between the three herons, but otherwise no sign of impending aggression, though all were rigidly wary while sizing each other up. The small female stayed within her chosen corner while the two males occupied center stage, stretching, folding, fluffing, and slimming their necks with a particular emphasis on a long diagonal lean that always brings giraffes to mind. During this tense semaphoric exchange of body language, they were so keyed up that when I coughed unseen at the window, the resident male, now standing on a low branch, bent slowly over, opened his beak widely, and regurgitated five fish in a shining heap.

An astonishing thing then happened. All five observers stiffened to instant attention: the first to move was one of the bitterns who crept forth with nervous glances up at the huge form towering over him and swallowed one of the fish! Then the new male stepped forward to snatch from the pile, and finally the little female, flashing her crest warningly, shot suddenly out of her corner straight into the middle of the group to grab her share, giving the bittern a cursory mock-blow as she did so. In about two minutes all those still-warm, well-travelled fish were redistributed in other stomachs. Even though now full-sized, the immature herons and bitterns regarded the act of regurgitation as an invitation to feed, as their parents used to do for them at the nest.

When the Legs Don't Work

When a bird's legs refuse to support him, the all-important question is: Is the damage to the brain or to the spinal chord? Just like people, a crushed midspinal chord leaves legs and other lower-chord functions totally paralyzed, or paraplegic, and paraplegia is permanent. If the damage is to the brain, the legs, especially if they have any tension or movement, will probably recover most of their use in two to four weeks. But it is not always so clear-cut, for early signs may be confusing, the birds cannot speak, and there are no diagnostic tests to apply. Slowly, experience has begun to give us a rough guide. But when we received our first Great Blue Heron crumpled pathetically on his side, unable to move his legs, I had already managed to nurse to recovery a few hawks and owls with leg dysfunctions and I thought, why not a heron? If I don't try I will never learn. So I tried.

Like so many others, this unfortunate heron had had a collision with a car or high wire, immediately paralyzing not only his legs but also his cloaca, the receptacle that in birds holds both feces and urine. Every two hours (except when he slept) I held him upright and gently massaged his cloaca to emptiness, cleaned and positioned him over a diaper in a tall carton filled with soft pine needles to support him as vertically as possible. To give him privacy, his box was in the gloom of the storeroom. Once each day I let him float weightlessly in the laundry sink and then blew him dry with my hair dryer; four times each day I sat supporting him between my knees, feeling like a parody of Santa Claus, and exercised his flaccidly dangling legs. While I was holding him, I took the opportunity to grasp his beak and slide down a few fish with minimal argument, for given all such unnatural conditions, he could not possibly feed himself.

At first he was so terrified at being handled that he was nearly unapproachable. Shrieking frenzied threats and stabbing wildly in a way that made contact tense and risky, patterning my arms with a crisscross of thin weals, I realized I was lucky not to have been struck in the head as well. But presently a most surprising change came about, perhaps because of his youth; he resigned himself to my consistent, predictable attentions so that after a few days he only signalled his anxiety by a slight cresting of his head feathers. Nevertheless, he continued to bite my hands and arms regularly, but now gently, as if in play: in the language of falconers, he had become "manned." This, however, only applied to me. He continued to strike fearfully at anyone else who passed within range.

On the third day I was encouraged by some jerky twitchings of his legs. Ironically, as they strengthened, he weakened, for the stress of his helplessness, the physiotherapy, bathing, drying, feeding, and positioning must have been nearly unbearable. But dammit, something was healing, for by the ninth day I was reassured to find that he was gaining bowel control and only needed help to empty it once or twice a day. This was a great advance, but simultaneously other parts of him began to wear out. First, his thin breast skin broke down because of the constant rubbing despite successive attempts to protect it with towels, quilting, sheepskin, and foam. Second, because he was of such a restless species, probably much affected by the stillness and isolation of his indoor surroundings, he flapped his wings a lot. Though this exercise was excellent for his system and probably prevented him from dying of hypostatic pneumonia, it unfortunately caused his wings to strike the edges of the carton repeatedly. All my efforts at padding could not prevent this, and all that padding produced an unexpected drawback. The tip of a heron's beak is edged with tiny, sharp backward serrations for gripping slippery prey, and when these kept snagging in the soft materials it panicked him, causing him to jerk about and flap harder than ever. As a result the undersides of his wings grew raw and I just had to get him out of that box. But how could I support him otherwise?

I tried a little psychology. Perhaps, I reasoned, he would flap less if he was under my eye more often and if he had something else to occupy his mind. I carried him out of his box to my office-cum-rodent-room and positioned him on cushions on the loveseat where he could watch mice romping busily about in their aquariums (we always breed a few lab mice for special occasions, and old aquariums make fine mouse-houses) and where I could in turn watch him. By golly, didn't he brighten up! And when he signalled intention-movements of wanting to flap, I would quickly lift him by the thighs and let him "fly" over my head where his big wings, flapping powerfully up near the ceiling, nearly pulled me off balance. He used to flap on and on till he was quite puffed out. This phase went on for a week and was so successful that his torn underwings healed over. He took more interest in food too, even beginning to "lick his lips" like the little bitterns when I rubber-gloved a perch for him, and attempting to mouth it, though he still could not swallow it until I stood him up.

Unfortunately these improvements were short-lived, for once again he became unendurably frustrated, and no amount of hoisting him up for "flying" seemed to relieve him. As soon as I had positioned him carefully back on his cushions he would begin to flap restlessly and lose his balance, dragging himself across the rug, battering his great primary feathers, abrading his skin, and opening new sores on his elbows. There was no curbing him, yet he was a long way from standing—in fact, though the nerves to his cloaca now worked perfectly, the small sputtering signs of life in the nerves of his legs seemed to have reached a plateau and had stopped altogether.

Then one night instead of sleeping quietly as positioned, he must have spent several hours crawling around, and as soon as I lifted him up I knew we had lost the long struggle. The thin skin over his breast was gone, and the underlying muscles split open irreparably. After seventeen days, he was exhausted and his spirit spent. Sadly, I gave him his permanent rest, and stayed with him as he drifted off into a sleep that deepened slowly into death. I had become very attached to this poor giraffe-bird and could only hope that my notes, photographs, and videotapes of his symptoms and progress might help in future cases of Great Blue Herons with legs that won't work.

CHAPTER 4

DUCKS AND GEESE

The Nine Tarbabies

At the train station near Kingston, the double set of tracks and an encircling road cut off a small pond from the bigger cattail marsh beyond the embankment. Despite the number of cars, trains, and people near the pond, ducks frequent it and occasionally even nest on it despite its shallowness. Here one hot May morning the large brood of a female Mallard hatched and the female began to lead her thirteen babies from the pond to the cattail marsh.

They negotiated the road safely, the adult crouching long and low as she led her skitter of brown-and-yellow downies. Sturdily they labored after her up a shallow bank to the tracks, scrambled en masse over the great iron rail that towered over them, and bounced into the shining pool of thick black oil between the crossties. Peeping in terror, all the ducklings were instantly ensnared. Flying back and forth and calling desperately, the female alerted a shocked official who hurried to help; four stuck only by the feet were freed and ran thankfully after their mother, while the rest were brought to us.

The opening of the carton revealed a heartrending sight. Nine unrecognizable blackened blobs wiggled weakly, stuck hard to the bottom of the box. Hurriedly we bundled each shivering, shocked duckling in a paper towel and packed them together in a covered pail placed on a heating-pad while we rushed about organizing solutions, paper towels, gloves, pans, and disposal bags. We had seen many birds die from smaller foulings than this due to toxic absorption through the skin as well as ingestion during agitated attempts to preen it off.

Quickly Robin and I took a duckling each and began the cleaning process.

First, we used mineral spirits to saturate and break down the thickest masses. Next, when duckling bottoms became recognizable, each little one was shampooed very gently with Sunlight dish soap, followed by a prolonged rinse under the warm tap while a brown stream of liquified oil poured endlessly into our bathroom basin. Then it was pat, pat, squeeze with towelling till the ducklings were as dry as possible, and finally they were set down under the warmth of the red brooder-lamp sun, accompanied by an arid desert breeze from my hair dryer. This first cleaning took two hours.

After their wash they looked so pathetic!

As often happens, the washing process had affected their balance, and at this stage, they looked *so* pathetic! Spiky and skinny beyond belief, shivering violently, staggering, some even lay helplessly on their backs waving their droll webbed feet feebly in the air. Their anguished piccolo-peeps continued undiminished for another hour as Robin stood over them, righting them and shepherding them gently together into the breezy mainstream of the chinook, while I cleaned up the sticky trail of brown-and-foam spatterings—the gunk was even in my toothbrush. When I finished, I heard the ducklings—no longer the shrill cries of distress but the soft chatty notes of conversation. I hurried in to see, and sure enough, they were now bright-eyed nearly yellow fuzzballs again, all on their feet and looking expectantly about for . . . I bounded upstairs to the kitchen for a glass pie dish, filled it with warm water, and handed them their pond. Instant action! Scrambling eagerly in, some sipped, splashed, and ducked with zest, while others preened busily around the perimeter. Though they would need to be "processed" once more, to judge by their spirits, they were certainly going to live.

Next morning found them all still spunky, though a lot more oil had flowed down from their skin and hardened on their bellies, so we did them again, finishing with a small tube-feed. This time, luckily, they hardly seemed to mind, and less than twenty-three hours after their admission we were at the station with the surprised officials, looking for the easiest way to clamber down the stone embankment to the edge of the marsh. Nine clean, waterproofed ducklings hurried out of the box and were immediately absorbed in marsh life, all busy with little-ducky dabbling and very charming they looked too. The mother Mallard could not be far away with the rest of the brood. Oh yes, she would find them as soon as the nine began to pipe up.

The Inflatable Merganser

This handsome tri-colored diver proved to be the antithesis of the relatively easy-going dabbling ducks we had become familiar with. Right from the start this peppery Common Merganser was prepared to argue and to defend himself, and he was not only a strong duck, but also a big one, weighing seventeen hundred grams—as much as a Great Horned Owl. Quite soon we practically forgot that he even had a wing fracture (a single midshaft radial break which heals nicely without any support anyway) as we clashed with his unyielding personality over the simple elements of food and water.

The Inflatable Merganser

He made no sound in the four weeks he was our guest, except the inflationary huff-huff of air under pressure as he blew himself up and hissed himself out at our approach. When this act of repulsion failed to vanquish advancing hands, his toothed beak flashed out to rake our flesh so fast we never saw it—ah, pity the luckless fish he marked down in the wild. Indoors, unfortunately, the only living things he marked down were us, for right from Day One he obstinately hungerstruck, refusing all fish, large or small, dead on a plate or alive in the bathtub. Soon we were driven to force-feed him, and I felt sure that the units of energy he used up explosively repelling our advances must have exceeded the units of energy produced by the dead fish and supplements we managed to push down his throat, that is, when he did not instantly give a headfling that shot the fish across the cage. He had bouts of violent strength, leaving us with wry recollections of arms bitten, walls fish-spattered, and rugs wet-stained in pursuit of our duties (and of the fast-running merganser).

Getting wet: the waterproofing problem again. It was January, so we provided the wherewithal indoors. Or tried to provide it. To start, he refused to bathe in his cage, so I tipped him into a full laundry sink; he assessed its limits, gave a mighty leap, crashed to the floor, and ran. A repeated introduction was foolish, for I was the only one who got wet. In the white upstairs bathtub, he floated listlessly while a school of shiners sheltered under his hind quarters, his only spurt of energy being when he left it. So it had to be our roomy Robin-built shower-tub, where the encircling walls of dark tile made a fine birdbath and provided privacy the merganser would appreciate. I filled it full, added an improvised sandbar, and kicking in furious frustration, in he went.

Judging by the ecstatic sounds coming from behind the shower-curtain — splashing noisily, scrambling out, plunging in — at last we had found the solution to his waterproofing problem, and we smiled at each other with relief. But I stopped smiling when it was "out" time and I realized this high-octane diver had no intention of being handled yet again. When I finally managed to capture his large slippery body, we were both equally sodden. How, I wondered as I changed my clothes and towelled myself, could this twice-a-day bathing business be terminated more gracefully?

Often it is the birds themselves who make plain a solution we cannot see. The merganser showed me the way out of this double bind (I hated getting soaked, he hated being chased) the next time by a happy accident. When I drew aside the curtain to pounce on him, he hurled himself straight between my legs and out of the bathroom, made a sharp right, tore through the next two rooms, wheeled right again and skidded into the laundry room, coming to an abrupt halt in the vacant heap of pine needles left by the pelican. Here, he settled down to preen, and adopted it for the rest of his stay.

His last revelation was his memory, for the next time he was "tubbing" he anticipated my return and took advantage of my first peek to repeat his racing lap all the way into the pine needles without missing a turn!

Thus were the twice-daily stressful captures eliminated, and instead, he provided entertainment for visitors near the finish line. They would see well-trained me go around the corner into the bathroom and say in dramatic lion-taming tones, "Go to your bed!" as I jerked open the shower curtain. A large, wet, and determined merganser would then race at full speed past them, his webbed feet slapping a rapid tattoo as he concentrated on his speedy slalom course, past the winning post and home.

Of Other Diving Ducks

Occasionally we have been presented with a few other deep-diving ducks such as scaup and scoters, familiar only by binoculars in their rafts far out on lakes and oceans. To begin with we were perplexed as to what we ought to feed them—till the first scaup took the matter in his own beak and showed me himself.

The scaup, who was sharing a large indoor cage with a Ring-billed Gull, had settled (resignedly, perhaps) for the dry food mix we usually offered to dabblers, but one day when I was offering a dangle of chopped skinned mouse on the end of forceps to the gull, the scaup leaned across suddenly and snatched it instead, gobbling it down with enthusiasm. Perhaps it was the movement of the meat that attracted him, but from then on—not surprisingly—he showed a clear preference for mouse over corn.

In summer, though scaup and scoters do eat a lot of water-plant parts including seeds, in winter, they raft up to fifty thousand strong on the Atlantic over mussel beds, enjoying a variety of animal life that includes clams they pick up on deep dives and swallow whole. So when we received our first artistically decorated White-winged Scoter one winter, a friend went to a lot of trouble to chop ice and find a few small clams for him; to our dismay the big black duck ignored them completely. What could I feed this strange creature? Then I remembered the scaup. Off to the kitchen I went and mixed up a plateful of egg yolk, lean ground beef, oystershell, and chopped mouse. To my amazement the scoter hurried forward and woffled down the mix so fast that I was still holding the dish in my hand. Thereafter, just the sight of one of us picking up the yellow-handled mouse-choppers was enough to bring him to the vertical wooden bars of his cage where he stood up as tall as possible and rapped eagerly on the dowels with his beak! This was astonishing behavior, not only because he was signalling his enormous appetite so clearly (he weighed 1,200 grams and ate 200 to 325 grams each day) but also because he was accurately interpreting our intentions before any approach was made in his direction. Of course, all birds are extremely sensitive to reading body language, but this duck responded more like an uninhibited puppy; probably his lack of fear was characteristic of all deep-water birds who keep such distance from the human race.

His positive personality, combined with his round black body, his scarlet, pink, and yellow beak edged with rows of rubbery serrated "teeth," and his brilliantly decorated eyes made him a memorable patient for the three long months he was here. Like many other waterfowl forced onto ice after a sudden freezeup, he had lost his vital waterproofing and unfortunately never regained it.

Everything has a purpose in nature, and I puzzled over the purpose of those striking white eye patterns—bold, sweeping Oriental brush strokes painted around his pale eyes. One day as I was watching him through the one-way glass in the wall just after he had eaten hugely, he relaxed into a pleasurable post-prandial siesta; but as he began to doze, his ivory irises seemed to grow bigger and more emphatic than ever—yet he was now asleep! The white comma pattern had expanded to include the closed eyelids, also vividly white when unfolded, so to a distant predator a flotilla of sleeping scoters may look very alert indeed.

The Goose Guest

Another bitter cold snap, another ice rescue. This time a small patch of rapidly freezing water contained a pair of Canada Geese, and binoculared onlookers could see that a wing of the female was heavily weighted with a mass of ice. Though the river's new ice was dangerously thin, two men set out to help, sliding a canoe between them—a long walk to the patch of brown water at the river center. It was penetratingly cold. Steam puffed from their faces, and shifting ice groaned ominously and cracked like sniper fire. Those huddled on shore watched tensely as the canoe sledded to a halt; and as the weakened goose was hoisted in, her frenzied mate honked and fluttered about them in fear and distress, not abandoning her till she had been bundled into a car and was out of sight.

Like that of the loon, the wing injury proved an old one. The ulna had been fractured by buckshot, but though the bone had healed, a major nerve had been damaged, paralyzing half the wing. Without sensation, the wing hung out and dragged awkwardly in the water, icing progressively, growing heavier, and dipping deeper. By the time she was captured and the large chunk of ice melted away, her wing was frozen solidly through. It is remarkable that sometimes frozen tissues in birds do recover, defrosting and dripping for days as did this goose's wing, though her flight would remain limited by the effect of the shot.

The new widow spent the last few weeks of that winter living with us, a lonely guest padding patiently about the house . . . it seemed unkind to cage her in, and besides, living on equal terms with a wild goose in your home is a good way to become familiar with such an elegant creature. This Goosess had an air of regality that endeared her to us, and we enjoyed her presence and forgave her her little green sins.

One dawning, Robin and I were still in the best place in the world—bed—when our drowsy peace was lightly invaded by the soft sounds of approaching feet. The steps paused at the open door, but no knock followed to show the respectful presence of an offspring. The feet entered. We simultaneously peered out from under the blankets to find that our visitor was the Goosess, headed for her first bath of the day. She walked unhurriedly past the end of our bed, into the bathroom, and leaped gracefully into the high-tiled tub. (Would that the merganser had done that too!) After a minute or two she stuck her head out and looked about. No water? she seemed to say. I quickly got up to put down the stopper and turn on the cold shower for her. Presently we heard the hissing downpour change in resonance as the goose moved into its center to allow the maximal thrust to rain on her broad back.

Meantime, though completely wild, she made some basic compromises about living with us, and we with her. After all, a free-walking, wary goose presented a number of small problems to which we found two solutions: one was Bissell's "Wall to Wall" solution diluted 1:8, and the other was to avoid making her nervous.

Geese are not only constantly with companions of their flock but also mate for life, and it was clear our goose was suffering incurable loneliness till quite by accident she discovered solace in the full-length bedroom mirror. The silent goose she found there was as curious as she, and approached till they unexpectedly bumped beaks. They were fascinated with each other, and we were equally intrigued by the repeated head signals she made, small circling motions ending with her bill pointed skyward. An unexpected facet of her understanding of "another goose present" came to light when, after investigating around the corner and failing to find the new goose there, our Goosess set about apparently trying to either get *in* or to let Solace *out*. Perhaps the edges and plastic braces of the mirror were the entry to Looking-Glass House, so for long periods each day she chewed them with drrrr-uming sounds, trying to remove the mirror from the wall. She seemed to think in relative dimensions.

Her loneliness was palpable. For a day, she even tried to commune with the deep-diving scoter whom she discovered living in the intensive-care room. Although they had had previous disagreements during mixed bathing in the cramped confines of the tub, grunting and biting each other, the goose later followed the scoter to his waist-high cage and settled down outside it, even putting her long neck between the wooden bars in order to get the most out of the companionship. The scoter was tolerant, but they were too foreign to each other to find more than some temporary distraction. But the unhappy goose tried to find enheartenment in one more unexpected way; she squeezed herself into the cramped dark space directly *beneath* the scoter's cage where the audible thudding of the big duck's steady heartbeat, amplified by the wooden floor on which he lay, was transmitted directly to her back. For three hours she crouched there; it was a moving sight.

Spring came, her wing now healthy but somewhat limited still, and we found a perfect place for her—a large pond owned and watched over by a couple who would feed and protect her in the coming winter if need be. Here, as she practised making short, low flights, scanning the skyflocks for others of her species, a Canada gander landed one day . . . and stayed to provide the authentic solace we never could.

*The Goosess
talking
to Solace*

kit Chubb

CHAPTER 5

THE STORY OF YIK

In a November of our early years, a box from Brockville yielded a matchless trusting creature who was to have a powerful and lasting influence on us.

From the darkness of the cramped carton she rose up, a calm and curious young Rough-legged Hawk who had been shot on her first southward migration from her subarctic homeland. Perching on the edge of the box, she looked about her with curiosity, projecting an aura of gentle fearlessness the like of which we had never experienced before, and seldom since. I mulled over the four reasons for raptor "tameness": first, being raised in captivity; second, the apathy of severe starvation or terminal illness; third, various cerebral damage, including blindness and retrograde amnesia; and fourth — this hawk's reason — the lack of a parentally imparted fear of man. This last is the classic response of those from relatively uninvaded wilderness, habitats such as the desert, the polar regions, and the tundra where the young may never glimpse a human being during their formative weeks and thus the parents cannot demonstrate and instil vital life-long man-fear. For raptors such as this one that must migrate into populated regions, this can be a fatal flaw. But for Robin and me, this lack in this beautiful northern raptor was to offer rare and invaluable glimpses of spontaneous and uninhibited behavior.

First we tube-fed her, though this is now a treatment we reserve only for the most critically emaciated who are too weak to swallow. Then there followed antibiotics, X-rays, and a veterinary operation to pin the humerus. While she was struggling through the anaesthetic aftermath she showed another unexpected reaction to us. Severe human pain is accompanied by cries, faints, and an inability to carry on normal behavior, for example, eating. In nature, it is in the bird's best interest to suffer, even to die, on their feet in silence, and in captivity pain is borne without a sound. But Yik had no natural inhibitions. Between groggy disorientation, pain, and God knows what horrors in her head, she lay helpless and miserable, crying like a lost and frightened chick. After all she was almost certainly only half a year old herself! I was so heart-wrung by her continuous cries that big hawk or no, I instinctively lifted her limp body from the cage and cradled her in my lap, whereupon she immediately stopped her distress calls and slept peacefully. Astonishing! No other hawk before or since has ever given out a single post-anaesthetic whimper. After an hour Robin took my place, but once again she began to toss and cry, "yik, yik, yik, yik," as soon as he tried to steal away; so for the next several hours she slept securely on alternating laps till she was steady enough to stand.

For the next month we gave Yik the most spacious cage and best possible care. This included three kinds of antibiotics, extra vitamins, and physiotherapy after pin removal, for something had gone dreadfully wrong and she could hardly open her wing. Like all birds she hated to be grasped, but unlike the rest, she let us know it by yikkering deafening protests throughout her passive exercises, though minutes after she was as friendly to us as ever.

Because of her extraordinary attitude to us all, it was unthinkable to keep her confined, and so her door was always open. People hearing of this often envision uncontrolled chaos, but this is never so; any bird free-flying in a home quickly establishes a routine defined by its preferences and limitations. Yik treated her cage as her personal retreat where food, bath, and perch were specially suited to her needs, but sought entertainment each day in my office. Here, she would jump to the back of her favorite chair to preen or even hop on my desk to perch on the platen of my old Underwood, even as the carriage trundled along. Ping! A peculiar leaden sensation. Sometimes she amused herself by watching "mouse-avision," whose busy occupants provided hours of rapt attention for us all. Her pupils dilated excitedly and her neck craned as small mice ate, yawned, and carried bits of nesting material about, but she was too well fed to actively covet them. When she had had enough she would run down the corridor to the intensive-care room and jump back up for the comforts of her cage.

To counter stereotyped "canary cage" concepts, it is essential here to describe what "cage" means at the Ark, particularly those designed and carpentered by Robin for raptors. No wire is *ever* used. The bank of five cupboardlike compartments is based on a long, deep waist-high shelf on the basement wall, fronted with sliding doors and divided by solid removable dividers. None are less than one hundred centimeters high. Within, they have fluorescent lights on the ceilings, astroturf mats on the floor, and "furniture" to suit the occupant. The doors are of two types: vertically dowelled varnished wood, or solid with peephole. All lift out for quick removal or exchange.

Yik's only neighbor was a Red-tailed Hawk found in Sandbanks Provincial Park, whose right brachial nerve had been damaged by a shot, causing a paralyzed, awkwardly dangling wing. Presently I withdrew the divider between these two long-term patients, thinking that companionship might add some zest to the long days of incarceration, and leaving Sandbanks free to explore if he wished. He had a naturally instilled fear of us, so we knew he would not venture far.

Portrait of Yik

Right away it became obvious that Yik was as uninhibitedly friendly toward her Red-tail cousin as she was with us, while Sandbanks was as wary and tense as wild hawks are when suddenly confronted at close range with a stranger. Undeterred by his stiffness, she hopped over within minutes and perched beside him—again, a most unusual approach. Following the long-established code of raptor politeness, they carefully avoided looking directly at each other, but their peripheral vision was in full use.

Presently it was evident

that Yik was troubled by that limp wing dangling so disjointedly, and she did an extraordinary thing: she leaned over, and grasping the carpal area with her beak, she raised the wing up and pressed it against the hawk's shoulder where it ought to have been. Sandbanks stared straight ahead till Yik let go and the wing fell with a jerk, making him glance around sharply. He had not felt the pinch of her beak, but only became aware of something happening when his body was jarred. Yik tried again and again, not giving up till she had made five more attempts which I managed to photograph. Was her sense of order disturbed by the wing displacement, or was she really trying to "help" Sandbanks? I tend to distrust anthropomorphic interpretations of behavior, even my own. Though there have been several reliable reports of birds helping each other, they were usually united by some bond of flock or family.

Yik adjusts Sandbanks's paralyzed wing

Yik showed fear of most fully grown owls. Once when we had an injured Long-eared Owl in the same bank of cages, Robin brought Romulus, our tame Long-eared Owl (whose story is to unfold later) into the room, riding on his fist. While we noted that the injured owl showed no apparent interest in Rom's presence, and Rom was preoccupied by an exciting sound somewhere else, we had not given a thought to the effect on the two watching hawks. Though both Yik and Sandbanks were each five times the weight of Romulus, they were simultaneously frozen in fright, their feathers bristling, trembling. Robin had to remove the little owl, who was calmly preening herself, apparently unaware of the unwavering stares of the two big buteos. Perhaps all owl shapes suggest the dreaded Great Horned Owls that threaten those that in darkness cannot see as well as they.

During the long six weeks Yik was in intensive care, frequent changes took place round her. The double cage she had shared with Sandbanks became an open triple so that it resembled a great shelf with bath and perches. Sandbanks himself never recovered from his wing paralysis and went on to develop aspergillosis for which we had to give him the Long Sleep, but in his place other buteo hawks in turn kept Yik company. One of these was a dark-phase Rough-legged Hawk, a beautiful near-black clone of Yik (though without the serenity) who looked thoroughly startled by Yik's abrupt and self-invited approach into his cage and onto his perch. Raptor politeness ruled: he made no objection.

After six weeks her wing still would not open, because of a "tie-down" of tendons entangled in the bony callus at the fracture site. When we realized sadly that Yik would never fly properly again, we stopped trying to stretch the wing and simply put her outside. This was now January.

A week later the weather had a little fit, offering a day of pouring followed by a night of freezing. Next morning I saw a glittering, hawk-shaped ice statue bent low to the ground—oh, Yik!—and I rushed out to bring the crystal-glazed creature in. Her waterproofing had been reduced by her long stay indoors so that her sodden plumage had rapidly rimed. As soon as she arrived downstairs she leaped up onto the back of her favorite chair and shook herself heartily, showering us with brittle tinkles of ice.

When settled and beginning to dry, Yik did a curious thing: she ran down the corridor to the intensive-care room and gazed up at the closed doors of her old cage. It was empty. Or was it? From its dusky depths a shadow silently detached itself and mushroomed into a Barred Owl peering down at her—a Frankenstein of horror to poor

Yik, who trembled and crested with shock. Rooted, she remained thus till I nudged the back of her legs onto my fist and whisked her away; it was about fifteen minutes before she recovered. Again it seemed to be just the "owl bogeyman" she feared, for Barred Owl ultralights, with their small feet, could pose no threat to such a hawk.

A month later I again brought her in because of foul weather—she looked half-drowned after three days of lashing cold rain. Oh, I know now she can tolerate any of the worst conditions far better than I can, but I worried anyway, and besides it would be diverting to see what she might do. She went through all the previous motions: "flew" down the stairs, scrambled onto the same chair, shook herself, preened and sorted plumage busily in the warmth of the wood stove, and then . . . that irresistible urge to go down the corridor to visit her cage one more time. I was on the phone when she left, so unluckily I missed her expression when she found it was occupied yet again, this time by a strange Red-tail. Presently rhythmic percussive thumps penetrated my other ear. What on earth was going on? I broke off and hurried to see. The invalid was perched in his cage looking startled, as well he might, for there clinging to the bars of his door was Yik, beating her big wings whump whump whump like some overgrown butterfly. There was only one response and I made it—I opened the door as requested and immediately she went in as breezily as any prison visitor, sprang on the next stump, and began preening again as casually as if they were old friends.

The memory of her cage has never faded. When she is brought in once or twice a year, even nine years later, she always goes to see it. Sometimes, if it's empty, she will jump in, an old guest habitué for a day or two. Room service, please.

Surely that's the equivalent of a three-star rating?

■   ■   ■

Though occasionally we had to divide it when we were full up elsewhere, once we had put Yik in the big central aviary it all soon became very much hers. Over the years she shared it with dozens of Red-tails and Rough-legs, up to five at a time; they usually accorded her first pick of the food. She also took her pick of the pools—how she did love to have a good wet! When one of us would begin spraying the hose to fill each newly cleaned pool, Yik would come running to be showered, pirouetting about with wings open, followed soon by repeated immersions in the bath. All the naturally fearful other hawks were too shy to be seen bathing; they took such pleasures in the privacy of dawn.

Generally these mixed buteos, following those ancient codes of politeness, got along quite amiably till the late summer of Yik's fifth year, when she built herself a nest and guarded it with amazing ferocity against all who passed near. Intramural trespassers were systematically knocked down and rolled over no matter how much bigger or stronger than she. At the first rumpus, we considered that she had merely taken a scunner to one she couldn't abide, but it became increasingly plain that there were none she could abide. In their best interests we had to house them elsewhere until Yik's annual inflammation had subsided.

She often accompanied us on walks through the woods, across the fields, beside the lakes, riding unleashed on one of our fists. Whenever she wanted to investigate something she simply leap-flapped off to explore till presently one of us would stoop to offer her the fist again. Though there were little creatures flitting and flying about, the only birds that drew her attention were other hawks soaring overhead — often soaring so high that they were mere specks to us, pinpointed by her tension and steadily cocked eye. Vultures were given only a glance; it was the buteos that got the long stare.

One of our regular summer routes was along a portion of windless, heat-shimmery railway track and through bush country to the edge of an unpopulated lake where the shady moss-bedded conifers were her favorite stopover. Robin and I would drop our clothes and dive off the high, hot granite rocks while Yik headed for the hemlocks to pad about the damp springy moss that cooled her feet and perhaps recalled her tundra origins. Once she deliberately flung herself in the lake, quite rapidly "sailing" a fair distance out. Robin, though a good swimmer, was afraid he might have to rescue her before she blew away, but no; believe it or not, she rowed herself back with her wings, floating lightly with every sign of relaxed enjoyment. (Years later she did this again when she was getting too much attention at a noisy July First lakeside festival. Fed up with the heat and crowds, she leaped into the lake and floated out of reach till she felt pacified once more.)

The only time the words "petulant" or "disputatious" could be used about her was once or twice when we were ready to go home from this spot and she wasn't. What a range of stratagems expressed her intention to stay! She ran off through the undergrowth in all directions, and refused to mount the fist; when she did mount she dug in her talons fiercely and rushed away again till finally we simply had to put her much-hated jesses on. Then she hurled herself off in a dreadful bate and hung upside down by the legs, refusing to perch ever, ever again. (All jessed hawks, falcons, and eagles bate occasionally from their perch or falconer's fist.) Yik's resolution proved implacable, and the only way we got her home was by carrying her in our arms — a violation protested by deafening distress calls ringing in our red ears every step of the way.

The approach to our house produced an unvarying reaction from her, even that awful day. She would tense up and then shoot vigorously off, running across the lawn and round the house to her aviary where we slowpokes would find her pacing back and forth outside, impatient to be let back in. Open my door. I want to go home.

■   ■   ■

Because of her fearlessness, she has been a veteran of many seminars, weekend educational conservation projects, Boy Scout camp do's, and so on. Judging by the alacrity with which she jumps into the car, she takes pleasure in the ride. Early on she found that the lowered whiplash support makes a ready and comfortable perch where, by stooping, she can keenly watch the passing show, her beak and soft breath tickling the top of my head all the way there.

Yik has been the star of at least fifty lectures, usually completely free of leash and jesses. Repeatedly she has taught us the value of the familiar. For such outings, Robin built her a tall three-legged stump topped with suede. As soon as she arrived in a lecture room or on a stage, gracefully riding high on a fist, she fixed her eyes on her special stump and leaped to it, and there she stood for the duration of the lecture. While people have constantly admired her patience and fortitude in standing quietly for long hours, stationary still-hunting is a natural part of life for buteo hawks.

After the talk, she would step back onto the fist of any stranger who invited her with a gentle behind-the-leg nudge . . . for a minute, anyway, long enough to imprint her graceful winsomeness on the mind forever. Perhaps someone — hunter, farmer, or youth — might be converted in that brief but magic moment to forswear ever shooting another hawk. If so, lustrous Yik, by that single backward step with her small warm feet, may have saved many lives.

■   ■   ■

Yik turned out to be excellent for television appearances too. When the secretary of the Kingston Humane Society asked me if Robin and I would be guests on their weekly TV program, I knew I was going to enjoy myself, for Lori was an adroit and charming hostess. Yik accompanied us as a matter of course (who knows, we might not have been invited otherwise!) and to reinforce my conservation message I also brought, hidden under a small blanket, a wiggly Something Else in a basket.

This cablevision studio was simple, high-ceilinged, and spacious, with a rink of shining floor and comfortable chairs arranged chatwise on an plushly carpeted dais. The two TV cameras were unobtrusive without the usual electric wires snaking underfoot, and the spotlights were permanently set into the ceiling so that their warmth was pleasant but not overpowering. The staff flitted mothlike about their tasks while we set up Yik's favorite perch to which she immediately jumped from Robin's fist. But before she settled, something startled her off and away she rushed, slithering at high speed across the slippery tiles, bowling nervous crew members aside, who perhaps thought she was after them. But soon she tired of the involuntary skating and allowed herself to be guided back onto the perch. Here the powerful floodlit "sunshine" began to warm her feathers and caused her to do something rarely seen: she turned her back to the lights, and spreading her wings and tail out to their fullest, had a brief hypnotic sunbath—such a riveting pose!—just as the filming began. By this time we were all settled in our chairs; beside mine was the basket in which the Thing had promptly gone to sleep.

Five-four-three-two-one, said the camerman's fingers silently and Lori led off, introducing us. I, in turn, introduced Yik, now preening, her head buried deep in a flamboyant spray of belly feathers. A lively prediscussed discussion proceeded to cover particular points the public repeatedly asked us about: that it is against the law to keep *any* wild bird or mammal, alive or dead, in captivity without special government permits; that Yik, like all wild birds, was not owned by us but was a responsibility for whom we were accountable. Yes, our hawks and owls, as well as herons, gulls, and crows, were fed mice but no, the mice were not alive, for our rodents were prefrozen from commercial sources. If you find an injured bird of prey, capture it, and call us at once. How to capture it? When the raptor is on the ground, cover its head so it cannot see you, and with its head facing away from you, press your hands firmly on its back and then down its sides till you can grasp the thighs. Worry about the talons, not the beak. Then pick it up and place it on an old towel or blanket in a large cardboard box. . . .

By this time I had quite forgotten the little gray sleeper but Lori, of course, had not. "Do you have a surprise for us?" she asked me mischievously, catching me off guard. I hurriedly grabbed the basket and tried to extricate the fuzzy creature gracefully, but of course its talons caught in the blanket, snagged my pantihose, and dragged up my dress. Finally it was free, wobbling on the carpet at our feet — a nestling Great Horned Owl.

I explained to Lori how the secondhand nest (built in an earlier year by crows or Red-tails, for these owls never build their own) had broken apart, causing two owlets to crash to earth, killing one; that when the survivor arrived at the Ark I had immediately given it to another Great Horned Owl to foster, a partly blind male with a broken wing; that despite his handicaps he had accepted the lonely baby. At this stage, I said, the owlet had not yet learned fear, but soon her new father would teach her to beware of mankind, their only enemy, until she could fly and before she was banded and returned to the wild. Thus the chat ran on. Meantime, the charming but indifferent baby squatted sleepily, absently chewing on my shoe just the way she nibbled on her foster father's toes.

Too soon, a silent hand signal from the technician told us that the time was about up. Oh dear, there was so much more I wanted to say! (We breakaway housewives, you know, do *so* enjoy the power of a captive audience after years of deaf ears at home.) However, we bid our farewells and retrieved the recumbent nestling while the screen credits rolled over Yik, now dancing lightly and flapping her wings as if on cue. She was an entrancing sight.

As we walked away, I looked back to make sure we had retrieved all our chattels. I saw only one thing left behind and it was slowly sinking into the pale beige rug — a healthy black-and-white donation from the little owl. At last sight, the two TV technicians (looking religiously picturesque) were on their knees with their heads bowed together in the shafting spotlight, scrubbing hard. Waving gaily, Yik and I left them at it. I didn't have the heart to tell them that it was permanent.

CHAPTER 6

THE HAWK FAMILY

An Oar for an Osprey

Still alive, something big thrashed and struggled desperately on the sunset-stilled surface of Desert Lake.

A teacher, enjoying the late July dusk by his cliff-side cottage, mentally cursed the extroverted occupants of a noisy powerboat as it roared away, but there in its widening wash, a victim had been left behind. Alerted, he raced down the steps to the shore where he shoved off a boat and rowed out to the frantic creature, which on approaching, he recognized with shock as an osprey. Long flailing wings beat feebly as the drowning bird made desperate use of his last strength to propel himself toward the boat. Instinctively, the teacher proffered an oar as they met, and without hesitation, the osprey frantically clawed his way up the improvised ramp and fell over the side, where he hunched miserably on the bottom, shivering and gasping. This time, the arrival of man was welcome.

Soon after Robin and I received his terse phone call, the teacher's tires squealed up our driveway. Inside a soggy blanket we found our first osprey, semiconscious, panting rapidly, and unable to stand. After he had been warmed, dried, and treated for shock, we examined him closely and found he had been struck on the head, causing brain damage and visual disturbance, as shown by the unevenly constricted pupils of his frightened yellow eyes. What else but the powerboat? Impossible NOT to know one had hit such a spectacular diver with a two-meter wingspan, but my mind recoiled from the thought of someone running it down purposefully. We were further dismayed to find that the osprey's crop was full, as this could only mean that the fish he was diving for was for his young. Could his mate provide for them in his absence?

Though we were helpless to feed the wild female, we soon found we did not know how to feed the injured male either, nor did other rehabilitators we consulted. All variations on the theme of "fishes in dishes" failed to trigger recognition of food because we had not considered the natural biology of the osprey. We shortsightedly thought that since herons, kingfishers, and ospreys recognize and catch live fish from water in the wild, and that since herons and kingfishers continue to recognize and catch live fish from containers of water in captivity, therefore the osprey would also. Wrong. Primary food-recognition stimuli originate in the nest; herons and kingfishers are presented their food under conditions quite different from those of ospreys. We learned to re-enact scenes from their early childhood when a parent osprey arrived and dropped a still-flipping fish onto the nest floor—the primal trigger being a *live, moving* one, preferably over ten centimeters, jumping on the ground nearby. Ospreys simply do not recognize live fish in a bowl, bath, or pool as being related to food at all.

In the days that followed, the osprey's brain damage compounded the feeding problem. He not only refused to eat because we were offering fish wrongly, but he was also highly distressed by our presence and handling, staring with pale fearful eyes and crying high, plaintive body-shaking grunts whenever we approached or even looked at him too long. Hampered as well by defective vision and damaged nerves for chewing and swallowing, his tongue often lolled uselessly out one side of his beak. Patiently, we helped him eat, gently pushing down about 250 grams of chopped skinned mice each day (fur may cause digestive impactions in those unused to it) which would provide a higher caloric value than the same amount of fish.

On the ninth day, he recognized food for the first time, and as with many exciting discoveries, it was a case of serendipity. A large shiner had leaped out of the osprey's big water pan onto the floor; Robin casually tossed it at the osprey, who went stiff with amazement and quite forgot that we were still nearby. A fish? He focused on it intently, waddled clumsily after the cartwheeling creature, and, following cautious consideration, leaned down and pinched it in his beak. A fish! Gratified, he passed it to his talons to eat it in crisp dainty bites and began to search myopically about for more.

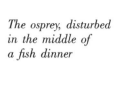

*The osprey, disturbed
in the middle of
a fish dinner*

To aid his fish-finding and his ungainly gait, his two-meter cage floor was entirely carpeted with green astroturf, for now obliged to walk about on those big curved talons as he never would in nature, he teetered as if on badly fitting high heels. Most of his time was spent firmly perched on a very low branch, though he learned to step off and bend awkwardly over to nip a fish as it paused in its death-dance over the floor. If it was too small to hold, he left it, just as he abandoned the tail ends of larger fish. No fish was ever swallowed whole. After his first tasty success, all fish in his cage, large or small, were acceptable, but only after he had identified them as fish. Until his eyesight improved still more, we had to put each corpse through a lively bump-and-grind routine with barbeque tongs; I even accompanied such resuscitation with off-stage splashing sound effects which developed a marked Pavlovian conditioning that was to prove useful later. I was much relieved when he lowered his standards to the inert corpses, as he needed at least six hundred grams of fish every day. Occasionally, he still ate a mouse by choice.

After two weeks, we put him in half of Yik's aviary. (Actually we tried him in with her first, but her response of horror was so dramatic that we hurriedly separated them.) There he crashed repeatedly into the solid plywood and plastic walls, shocking us by this demonstration of his bad eyesight. A splendid flagstone-edged pool with trickling hose seductively gurgling, he ignored altogether, disappointing me deeply. The daily indoor misting he had received was such a feeble substitute for a bath that I suppose I envisioned him galloping gleefully into the pool at a dead run. What an awful day it turned out to be! He ate nothing, avoided the water like poison, and at dusk was still trying to fly through the panel of his choice.

For the next two days I abandoned all pretense at housework and concentrated fully on finding a way to get him to eat, for being outside reestablished and worsened the problems of before: he could neither recognize fish at a distance, nor allow me to offer them close up. A person walking by was an intolerable threat, causing him to hurl himself at the farthest panel, and when it was a plastic one, he usually hung upside down till the plastic slowly ripped under his needle-sharp talons, and he dropped with a whump. When I went into his aviary he panicked still more—bad for him, not so safe for me either if he were to land on me by accident. With difficulty, I managed to spread out a roll of familiar green astroturf on which I dropped large colorful sunfish, but his dim vision did not recognize them yet. I tried flipping them onto the fake greenery while clanging my tongs and splashing up a water-bucket storm at the same time; though he clearly understood "food somewhere," he could not locate it. At sunset of the second day I went in, crawling low to minimize alarm, and wearily collected all the smelly sun-dried corpses. Would I have to take him back inside? I decided to give him one more day, though I hated to leave him harried, hungry, and still dry.

The clanking, splashing, and fish-flinging went on and on the next day as if some invisible director kept ordering retakes. The bewildered osprey gave anxious whinnying grunts at the food cues, but could not find the fish. Just when I was about to howl with frustration, a second lucky accident occurred: I did a "clang-splash-fling," and my fish-missle hit him on the foot! He peered nearsightedly at his attacker, gripped the welcome shape, and fell to at once. By the end of the day he had found four such treasures, and we both felt restored.

As he gained confidence and his eyesight got sharper, the scenario did improve. He began anticipating his meals till the mere prompt of Bucket-Tongs-and-Me would set him off, calling loudly and "smacking his lips" as all raptors do when stimulated by thoughts of refreshment. As I was his only attendant, he became familiar with my routine and resigned to my presence. We came to a compromise. Though still apprehensive, he learned to stand his ground and take a fish directly from my hand, providing I arrived slowly on my hands and knees.

It didn't rain for eleven days. I worried about this fresh problem, for waterproofing is quickly lost and slowly regained in captivity. When he continued to avoid the pool (even after he skidded in once by mistake), I made him preen and sunbathe with my little garden hose which rained coldly on him at a fixed time each day, creating lovely little rainbows all about. But on his fifteenth day outside, I woke to straight-down rod rain, and found the osprey right in the open, apparently as drenched as I had dreaded; astonishingly, as I watched he walked awkwardly over to the pool and had a *magnificent* bath. I then fed him (though the splashing in my bucket was inaudible over the drumming downpour), and hardly had I gone back indoors to the window when he proceeded to have two *more* ecstatic baths. Still in the rain he then assumed the spread wings-and-tail posture usually seen in drying off, as if he just couldn't get enough!

In mid-September, when from the highest perch he could now focus on small fish swimming about in the pool, we thought it best to release him. While one pupil was still contracted (probably from displacement of the lens) overwintering with us was unthinkable, and the average departure date for osprey migration in our area loomed only four weeks away.

So on a day resonant with sun and wind, we banded, weighed, and returned him to his own lake from the teacher's cliff top. As he climbed out of his box onto the grassy bluff beside us, his every sense locked fast to the water below, man unheeded, fear forgotten, remembering . . . readying . . . renewing. After a long concentration he tensed, unfolded his long wings to lift gracefully into the updraft— free—and flew steadily and purposefully across the shining lake.

Our osprey was surely headed home.

Harriers: After the Haybine

Early summer used to be a busy orphan season for us. During a sunny, dry spell, whole families of baby harriers were brought in because their homes in the hayfields had been suddenly scalped by a haybine. Formerly we accepted the healthy along with the injured, believing that the harrier parents could not cope with such a devastating loss. It was before we learned how protective and resourceful the adult female could be . . . and how successful, especially with a little help from the farmer. Though we didn't know much, raising harrier chicks taught us a lot.

Ground-nesting has always been their preference. Where possible they build in tall weeds or reeds near low meadows and swamps, but with shrinking marshlands and expanding grainlands, hayfields have come into popularity. Here, undisturbed and cool in the chest-high grasses, the woolly café-au-lait babies—as many as six—hatch on consecutive days and illustrate an amusing sequence of development. While the youngest is on belly-and-hocks, uniformly clad in cottony honey-fluff, the eldest is running rapidly about on long yellow legs with newly irrupted rust-brown plumage, leaving the fluff only haloing the head and stubby-tailed rump. Brown-eyed sisters are always clearly larger than their gray-eyed brothers. I'm not sure how the mother manages her brood of fast-snatching, high-metabolism young, but in captivity with us at feeding time, the smaller males are frequently dwarfed by the larger front-line females who often tread repeatedly on their low-profile siblings, forward in hunger or backward in fright. However, the males here have shown more and earlier initiative in attempting to hunt.

After the stage of hand-feeding skinned-chopped-mouse-on-forceps had passed, we would put them in large sheltered aviaries where, in the second stage, they learned to recognize and possess dead mice tossed on the aviary floor. Harriers always seem to be ravenous (with such high metabolism they need to eat at least one-quarter of their body weight each day). Our fledglings were alert with anticipation at feeding time when I would open the door to throw in large handfuls of little corpses and then retreat to the one-way window to watch. Soon I noticed that the mere opening of their door produced a demonstration of conditioning: the harriers quickly flew to the ground and began to run tensely this way and that, kakking loudly with heads down and wings and tails in full mantling position, exposing their white rump-patches. Mantling is a warning to other hawks about the possession of food in the foot, and is usually done standing still with the wings and tail spread in a wide semicircle to conceal the sight of the prey. In this case, not only was there no sight or sound of prey, but each harrier was quite empty-footed!

The third stage was to allow them to learn at least a few fundamentals of the hunt before releasing them. This seemed a good idea,

*A harrier
describing an
empty mantle*

even though the mice were tame and in unlikely vegetation—and were probably offered unnaturally early to the fledglings, whose parents in the wild continue to drop prey to their young late into summer. I arranged a low, wide pile of hay in the middle of the aviary, and each day I put a partly opened little box containing a dozen dark and docile mice under the hay, along with plenty of seed; some would soon escape from the aviary but others would become established there. The box provided a familiar-smelling home base and also slowed down their excited exit from the hay-pile until the highly nervous harriers had recovered from my intrusion.

The fledgling novices, perched high above, remained unaware of their opportunities for over half an hour, preoccupied with preening, dozing, and occasional swift light forays here and there; one even ran past the setup without a sign. They were not really hungry. However, a male eventually became attracted by the busy rustling and cautiously came to investigate. He was soon magnetized by the unexpected subterranean activity (even I could see the hay heaving and the occasional mouse showing itself) and stayed to find the cause. In this he was successful, but only in finding them, not catching them!

He jumped up onto the hay and stood splay-legged, head cocking about rapidly as he listened to the activity beneath. Presently, a whiskery nose poked out nearby, and when the mouse innocently joined him on the top in full view of his fascinated gaze, he stood stock-still as long as it did. The instant it scampered, he pursued, but as it was far faster than he, there followed a droll chase through the vegetation all the way to the far end wall and back with no danger whatever to the mouse. I'd have bet it wasn't even breathing hard. The other harriers perching overhead made those look-listen head movements indicating their attentive observation of the chase, but none joined in.

Presently the male returned to the hay-pile—still on foot—and set about discovering and uncovering the rest of the livestock. Several were playing about under the hay and he exposed them one by one by kicking away the hay with his foot, but without any idea what to do about them. His instincts told him he should do something about them but what? First he tried to pick one up with his beak but no mouse, however naive, is going to stand still to be pinched. Perhaps with the foot then? He grasped one gently thus, but it slid out easily between his toes and stood motionless before his perplexed gaze for nearly a whole minute before hopping away. On the third attempt he struck out with his foot correctly, but missed, lost his balance, and fell clumsily onto his chest. After a few more practice swings that rewarded him only with grabs of hay, he finally lost patience and flew up to join the others. It was not until two days later that I was sure of his success at last, announced to all the occupants of the Ark by his roisterous kakking of triumphant excitement. This time he was not empty-footed.

But as almost always, it is best for healthy babies to remain with their parents, and the following story shows how resourcefully one harrier mother managed her family after the remorseless advance of the haybine.

Bill's Way

A salesman who preferred the solitude of an old stone house set in the midst of acres of quiet hay fields spent much time with binoculars investigating the love life of his nearest neighbors, a certain pair of Northern Harriers. In spring he watched the courting male sky-dancing for his mate who soon built a nest in one of those same hay fields, and the man called Bill became caught up in their lives and protective of their interests. So when the farmer-landlord made preparations to mow the field and the young had not yet flown, Bill called us anxiously. How could he save the babies without disrupting the family?

Well-known studies by American naturalist Dr. Frances Hamerstrom have proved that if their babies disappear, harrier parents abandon their territory within twenty-four hours. So together we agreed that if Bill could persuade the farmer to leave an untouched "island" of standing grass around the nest, Robin and I would go at once to help capture and band the young before the mowing, and replace them immediately after. It was to be our first experience with harriers in the wild.

Thus it was that on a sunny July afternoon we three found ourselves slowly stalking, heads bent, through a chest-high hay field. The warm scent of the grasses enveloped us in the still summer air while our ears were filled with the soporific zigging of a thousand grasshoppers. At the edge of the field, the unmanned haybine hulked ominously, spurring us to our search while the female circled overhead, kakking a warning. Her nest—usually a more constructed effort—was simply a flattened area bestrewn with tufts of baby down, quite empty of little occupants, but Bill was not disconcerted. "They're hiding nearby," he explained. "See all these little trails? The little guys make them by running through the grass, but they freeze if you get close so they're hard to see." I was amazed by the numerous thin lines radiating erratically from the nest and vanishing into the deep grass everywhere. Bill found a large female chick almost at once. "OW! She got me right through my glove!" cried Bill, surprised, looking at a hole in his hand. Just then I too found a female; both were feathered, though their half-grown flight feathers were still "in blood." My catch was so apparently docile that I forgot myself and attempted to feel her crop with a fast finger, but her foot was faster still and thus Bill and I bled together for the cause, sucking our bleeding fingers and grinning ruefully at each other.

It took over an hour to find the last two well-hidden chicks, both males, but finally we finished examining and banding the foursome, showing Bill the surprisingly big ear hidden behind the owl-like facial ruff, and pointing out how much sturdier were the tarsi and "ankles" of the females compared to those of the smaller males. Presently, a dust cloud growling along the dried earthen road heralded the arrival of the farmer, who, now well informed, hailed his little mousing allies

and assured us he was quite content to forgo the hay around the
nest. As dusk fell before the mowing was completed, Bill tucked the
harrier chicks (each still full-cropped) overnight in the trunk of his
car, for we feared the well-trampled "island" was too freshly redolent
of human footprints to be truly safe from nocturnal four-legged
predators.

Up with the dawn like a true countryman, Bill straightaway replaced
the baby harriers in the "island" and settled to watch the action. Half-
a-coffee-cup later the adults sailed into view and performed the skilful
partnered aerial maneuver called "transfer"–the male above dropping
his catch, the female below rolling over to seize it neatly with her
feet. She then rewarded all Bill's efforts by taking the food to her
newly banded chicks, and in our view, Operation Haybine had been
a success.

The female, however, did not see it that way. To her, the site was
no longer safe, and next morning Bill phoned in considerable agitation:
she had marched all her chicks into the next field! Well done, O hawk,
but you could not dream that haven of grass was to fall that very
day. After a lengthy discussion we elected Bill to recapture them all
and move them back once more to the old nest site till the haybine
was done. This he did, though it proved a more formidable task than
before, as the new runways were faint—and worse, some of the chicks
were now able to spring into short bursts of flight. Once again Bill
guarded them while the second field was shaved without incident,
though the farmer was by now so concerned that he kept getting off
his machine to check ahead. Once again, we were all gladdened
except you-know-who, for by the next sunrise the vigilant mother had
moved them for the second time. Bill's binoculars found her feeding
them in a brand-new place, a small fenced-in spot that would
thankfully never be mowed.

They thrived. We knew in enthusiastic detail just how they thrived,
for throughout the summer Bill continued to send reports of their
progress, noting that well into August the immatures could still be
seen receiving prey from their father, though now by lofty aerial
transfer to them. This suggests that the immatures do not become
self-sufficient hunters till rather late, and till then, they need the
uninterrupted team support of both parents. It is my hope that
many farmers will hear of this story and try to help the harriers
Bill's way.

The Half-brained Hawk

One of the most baffling cases of brain damage we ever had was a little Broad-winged Hawk, the smallest relative of the Red-tails and Rough-legs. Her balance was badly affected, causing her to lean heavily back on her tail, and whenever she became alarmed by my approach, she would be seized by a violent fit that would cause her to fling about the ground clockwise. The rest of her time she simply stood on the floor in a kittenish pose with her head cocked, unable even to mount a stump or perch for the basic comfort that all healthy raptors enjoy. The head tilt was characteristic of partial blindness, and indeed she had no vision in the left eye and very little in the right, though the pupils reacted normally and the eyes appeared outwardly undamaged.

These symptoms were bad enough, but soon there proved to be one far worse. The small hawk showed no response of any kind to food: not to a still-hot mouse offered to her beak or placed on her foot, not to fresh bloody mouse liver placed in her mouth, not to a live mouse in her sight, not to another hawk noisily crunching next door (and she was not deaf). That was our entire repertoire of appetite-stimuli, and as each one left her completely blank, she had to be lifted out everyday to have chopped mice pushed over the swallow reflex at the back of her tongue. Throughout the first eight weeks, she exhibited this deeply entrenched amnesia for everything to do with appetite, recognition of food, and the act of eating. I thought of her when I read the absorbing book, *The Man Who Mistook His Wife for a Hat*, by American neurologist Dr. Oliver Sacks, when he spoke of a neurologically blind patient. "He was bewildered when I used words such as 'seeing.' He had lost all visual images and memories totally . . . his entire lifetime of seeing, of visuality, had in effect, been stolen . . . he had become, in essence, a non-visual being." The hawk had apparently become a non-nourishable being in the same way; her lifetime of eating had too been stolen, till one day when her damaged memory function was stimulated in a most unexpected manner.

Robin and I had just finished pushing down the daily meal—the fifty-sixth—and we were less careful than usual and overfilled her crop. As soon as she was put back in her cage, she threw up the whole lot of white-furred mouse chunks on the dark green astroturf floor. Peering down with great intensity at the scattered scraps at her feet, she made a profound and miraculous coupling in her disordered brain at last, and hesitantly, she began to pick them up and swallow them down again!

Thereafter she managed to recognize and to clumsily eat chopped white mice on a dark background but continued to be troubled by greatly limited vision and amnesic loss of early learning. As well, she was also troubled by poor motor skills, fumbling and dropping bits often, and when offered a whole mouse, she would spend long periods beaking it this way and that with no idea how to go about tearing it up. There seemed to be a faint and flickering stimulus to "do something" hawks do with mice, reminiscent of the young harrier who had no parental guidance to grasp his first live mouse. Nevertheless she managed just well enough to be put outside in a small aviary, even learning to climb up on a low perch, but unfortunately that was the extent of her progress after another eight weeks.

On postmortem her brain was a bizarre sight. The entire left half of the cerebrum was missing, lysed away by infection introduced through a depressed fracture on the same side of the skull. With it was gone the area behind the eye that pertains to feeding. The hawk must have been almost totally blind, for the visual pathways cross over in the brain of birds as in man, making it unable to transmit much to the good eye due to progressive loss of the left cerebrum. Ironically, though the right brain was able to transmit for left-sided vision, the retina of the left eye had been destroyed.

About Starvation

Our understanding of Rough-legs comes mostly from more than a decade with Yik, with only a few others of her kind ever in our care. Conversely, our understanding of her cousin Red-tails comes from a continuous stream of wounded ones, none of which stayed more than a year. These hawks breed more successfully than other buteos such as the Broad-wing and the rare Red-shoulder because they are more adaptable to available prey and nesting sites; on the other hand, being larger and more numerous, many more get in trouble from gunshots, leghold traps, and car collisions. Raised in populated latitudes, all are naturally fearful of man, and so after a debilitating injury, many conceal themselves until they starve.

The word "starvation" conjures up Third World images to most of us. Among wild birds, however, it is so pathetically commonplace that it is always the first thing we check for. At least a third of our birds of prey come to us so severely famished that for some the deprivation to fragile internal tissues is irreversible. Yet some of the most desperate ones sometimes manage to survive.

■   ■   ■

A cardboard carton opened to expose a young Red-tail, head bowed in weakness and apathy, so far gone that he no longer cared what strange things were happening to him. He made no move when I picked him up, bare-handed, and felt his chest; sure enough, the keel of his breastbone stuck out like a razor. His falling body temperature could be read by the decamping of his clan of feather lice, now clinging uneasily to the tips of his chin feathers, plainly saying they found it chilly at the roots of the feather-forest and who turned off the central heating anyway?

Immobile, the hawk's bone-pale eyes flickered as fingers searched over his body to find the cause. A fracture? A dislocation? A concussion? Probably the latter. Luckily he was not dehydrated as well. Practiced hands then placed him on his back on the scale where he lay as if stuffed while we read the evidence: 695 grams for a male (by our data, if it had been a female, she'd be dead). Yes, we *had* saved a few so emaciated. Be quick. Could he eat?

In a warm cage, we gently propped him up with towels, for he could hardly stand, and with forceps I quickly offered a fresh still-warm bit of mouse liver. Absolutely no reaction. Pushed it inside the partly gaping beak, where it was faintly mouthed and dropped. Poked it in again, and now, with a faint electric thrill of recognition, he tasted it, lifting his head to actually look at us for the first time. The second liver chip was accepted faster, and the third he reached for. Such a promising revival of the spirit! But let me not be tempted to overfeed him at first, though there are few things as gratifying as giving nourishment to those in need.

When he finished the bits of that little mouse, he had swallowed only 20 grams; a mere hors d'oeuvre for a bird who needed 120 grams/day, and who could pack away 200 grams at a meal. But resolutely I turned away from the starving hawk, giving him peace in the safe semidarkness. Instantly he was asleep, his head incongruously dangling, too exhausted to even tuck it under his wing.

The second mouse-serving an hour later was a different story. He woke startled, confused by the human presence, but then recollection flooded him. These hands meant *food*. Frantically impatient, a swift yellow leg shot out, crisply seizing the white Styrofoam dish of fresh "chops" over which he huddled low, gobbling each piece with that pathetic combination of pitiful weakness and desperate primal need.

Returning to his one-way window thirty seconds later, I watched him scrutinize the dish, barren, speckless, white. All gone so fast? He checked the floor for any missing morsel, carefully cleaned imperceptible fragments from his talons by passing each through his beak, and finally feaked his beak clean on the perch as healthy hawks do. Then calling on his newfound small store of strength, he struggled up onto the perch, buried his head comfortably into the rekindling warmth beneath his feathers, and retired into sleep again.

The lice retired too.

The Hawk That Came Back

Inexperienced Red-tailed Hawks are such frequent inmates here that it was not unusual late one August to find ourselves caring for three, all in a row, each calmly suspended in his own springy pine-needle bed, watchful, wary, patient. Coincidence: all paraplegics, all hit by cars, all full-sized juveniles, and thanks to their natural disposition for hours of motionless still-hunting, all a snip to nurse compared to the Great Blue Heron. While two were to progress uneventfully, the third—the one from Cornwall—unexpectedly distinguished himself. It is his story that follows.

As he rose heavily after a triumphant kill in a nearby marsh, a passing car bashed him broadside, bruising his spine and breaking his ulna, but despite the shock and pain, he tenaciously hung onto his newly captured muskrat. If he couldn't gain altitude rapidly enough, it is hardly surprising when one realizes he weighed eleven hundred grams—while his prize, dragging like a kedge, weighed about seven hundred grams!

After a week, he had regained use of his legs and could stand, limp, and feed himself, and so he abandoned his nest-bed for a proper perch. Free to exercise indoors, each day he practised walking to my office-cum-rodent-room, where he would jump onto the old love-seat cushions, and like Yik before him, watch mouse-avision. Visitors were rather taken aback, but Robin and I came and went nonchalantly about our business; why should a large hawk not be sitting tranquilly on our sofa if it pleases?

Comeback with paralyzed legs the day he arrived

Our home has harbored many such less-common relationships. There develops an unspoken understanding between ourselves and these big birds of prey, with elemental rules for us: move gently, speak softly, don't stare; be consistent in dress and address; keep your hands to yourself. In return, these truly wild hawks allow us to treat them in what must be a bizarre imprisonment to them. Simply put, we reduce their stress as much as possible, while they control their terror as much as possible. Both parties do a lot of reading of the other's thoughts; ours from experience of several hundred wild hawks, theirs from a razor-sharp intuitive awareness of our minute, unconscious body signals.

Such peaceful compatibility seems to speed healing. In less than five weeks from his unlucky hunt, the Cornwall Red-tail flew free from a small rocky cliff overlooking Howe's Lake, a twelve-minute drive away from us. As he sailed effortlessly off over the marshy inlet below, we wished him a safe migration, little knowing that in three weeks he would be in our hands again.

■   ■   ■

I knew something unusual was happening outside when all four of our kestrels began to scream. Very reliable watchdogs, they are, whose present pitch of alarm meant a big predator was close by, and just to underline their observation, Yik now turned on her siren wail— "it" was clearly in her view as well. After searching the well-wooded areas around the raptor compound without success, I had returned to the kitchen to finish getting dinner (damn meals) when a movement out the window caught my eye. There, right on top of Yik's aviary, stood a Red-tailed Hawk! He was walking back and forth over the chain-link, looking down intently . . . and trying to get *in*. As I watched, agape, he flew down into the little courtyard and began to search along the periphery for an entrance. I rushed out, whipping off my sweater as I went, but approached him quietly. On seeing me, instead of flying away, he tried harder than ever to butt through the chain-link wall, making no protest as I covered his eyes in order to grab his legs safely. Good grief, he was banded. I carried him into the treatment room, thinking hard.

Immature tail in October, so hatch-year hawk. Familiar with the aviary . . . a release of mine, but where from? He was amazingly calm, allowing me to examine his keel. Ah, lost some weight lately, have you. Why is the underside of your tail caked with droppings, old fellow? No self-respecting hawk allows that to happen. Let's feel your wings . . . aha, old healed fracture here . . . got it, you must be the Cornwall paraplegic. Oy, what's this? Blood? Holy cow, you've been shot half a dozen times through your lower back—no wonder you haven't hunted recently. Holes quite big too, feathers driven in deep, what a swollen mess of green bruising. Another hunter's target. There, you patient stoic, wounds all cleaned up. Now let's add antibiotics . . . rinse with Rogarmycin, powder with Tetracycline, squirt some DMSO superhealer over it all. Oh, and your Septra. Open up! Thank you. Hawks swallow pills so nicely. You shall be weighed, and have an X-ray too.

Now where am I going to put you, for all the intensive-care cages are full of other hunting-season targets: Cooper's Hawk, Red-tail, Broad-wing, Great Horned Owl. Oh well, let's use this corner cage for now. It'll be hell getting you out of it tomorrow, but by then I'll have moved the Cooper's out. There, how do you like that cage, dear fellow? You look surprised . . . of course, you were never in one; last time you squatted in a box on the floor, healing those paralyzed legs and that wing. Well, in response to that very expectant look, the moment we've all been waiting for, ladies and gentlemen — MICE. Wow! Snatch, stuff, gobble. More! More! That's what you came back to the Ark for, isn't it? Cupboard love, 'tis all.

When Robin and I had released him about seven winding kilometers away, he had travelled shut in the usual cardboard box on the car seat, unable to see anything. So how did he find us, or was it purely luck? My guess is that after the buckshot put paid to his hunting he remembered his well-fed five weeks here. He probably oriented himself by the frequent flights of our pigeon flock, with whom he was very familiar, having been in one of those very aviaries upon which they so nonchalantly loafed and sunned themselves. If he had been soaring high overhead he would have recognized the aviaries themselves, and doubtless some of the inmates (and with such excellent eyesight, what they were having for breakfast too). He would have recognized Yik's startling crescendo, which carries a long way, and finally, he might easily have heard the shrill smoke-alarm call of one of the sharp-eyed kestrels. Thank goodness for them, or he might be out there still.

Comeback recovered rapidly and was re-released in two weeks.

The Story of Left and Right

Up until now, all of our Red-tail admissions had been full-grown and injured; it was thirteen years before we saw a healthy nestling. Here is the story of two babies we raised one summer, of the work and worry that went to them, and of the pain and pleasure that came from them. Though we usually manage to persuade people to leave the young with the parents, this time we *had* to take them: their nest was on a quarry lip, about to be blasted.

They were large and timorous babies, rearing back skittishly when approached. Both were fluffy at each end with real feathers sprouting in the middle, and I guessed brother and sister by the difference in their ankles and feet — hers were noticeably more brawny. We cleaned out their ears, deafened by squirming fly maggots as usual. (I have come to suspect that this common occurrence solves itself naturally when the maggots drop out to pupate on the ground, the only residual signs being dirty ears, though occasionally — especially in the more capacious ears of owls — ulceration may develop.) Each cleansing completed, we handed them over to a newly appointed foster mother who was being treated for damaged feet in an aviary outside; the great pine-needle container on which she rested made a welcoming nest, and she adopted them at once.

The new family bonded strongly. Despite record heat their bodies stayed snug-packed for two weeks till the young hawks, becoming restless for adventure, began "branching" from the nest. As soon as they were perching confidently, we provided a short survival course like that for the harriers but surprisingly, this time it was the sister who pounced and chased with quickness and accuracy while her brother watched, yet later their abilities appeared equal.

By the twenty-sixth day they were enjoying newfound flight. It was disappointing not to be able to return them to their real parents (who had probably been driven from the nest area by the upheaval of quarrying) nor to be able to release their foster mum with them, for her feet were not yet healed. The fledglings must make do with our support instead, in the form of a hack here. We banded them, the male on the left leg, the female on the right, and propped the aviary door open for the start of their hack.

Several hours passed before they plucked up the courage to venture out, and then they stuck close together, only a flap away. Presently they slipped into a nearby thicket and I hurried to put fat dead mice on their aviary roof, thinking that if they did come back (oh, the anxiety! for they must, to survive) they would naturally be drawn to their old "nursery" enclosure.

Wrong thinking. They were drawn to their foster mother, who had been taken indoors for foot surgery when their hack began, and whom I had just put back outside five days later—not in the nursery aviary but in with Yik and another Red-tail. Though songbirds had daily informed us that the young hawks had not strayed far, it seemed significant that they never once came down to eat while their mother was absent. Was the mouse-heap on the nursery aviary hidden from a distance by abundant leafiness?

Soon after putting the adult out I ran to the window, alerted by bird-fuss and hawk-talk, and hurray! There stood Left on the chain-link roof of Yik's aviary, "yeeap-yeeaping" noisily down to his foster mum, while the hawks within answered with equal animation. Even Yik got excited and ran back and forth, adding a high wavering warble to the chorus. Immediately I scrambled up a ladder to put a generous heap of mice on this roof, though of course Left flew off long before my head popped over the top. But note was taken and later back they came. It was such fun watching each take turns kangarooing enthusiastically over the roof with comic exuberant leaps, snatching a mouse in *each* foot and bounding off again on closed "fists." They were extremely hungry.

After that, coming for food became a routine. Right and Left alternated, usually eating their selected feasts — about five big mice each day — on the roof directly over the residents' heads, where illogically, instinctively, despite the barrier of chain-link, each free hawk mantled warningly all through the meal. Both were seen regularly in the neighborhood, blatantly favoring — of all things! — television aerials, where they were made conspicuous by an ever-present retinue of small, feathered scolds that burst into renewed vituperation whenever a hawk made the slightest move, however innocent. (After some weeks the robins continued scolding out of habit, but I noticed with amusement that they now did it from the same aerial the hawk was using!) Of course the young hawks would not have picked such perches if they had had proper parents to guide them. I went from window to window, watching and worrying that a car, gun, or trap would find them.

It happened at last. Left was in trouble. When he flew he trailed a broken leg, and when he landed he teetered awkwardly, trying to balance with his wing, making himself more conspicuous than ever. Grounded and frustrated, I paced about our property, binoculars in hand, unable to help, for he was far too wild for us to approach him. But just once, he approached us. It was late in the second day when there was a tapping at our window and there to our astonishment was Left, sprawled awkwardly across the sill, his head against the glass, clearly showing us his dreadful leg. The action was so unusual that we knew he must be in a fearful state of illness and pain, but at our first move to reach him, he leapt up and fled.

On his third day Left collapsed on the aviary roof, looking miserably weak and exhausted, but even in that state he would not let us get near. Instead I noisily splashed cold water to fill the nearby big concrete pool in the lawn, hoping he might come to bathe as his sister had done the day before, for a fierce heat wave was in progress. To my delight he came down as soon as I left and had a refreshing bath. But time was running out for him. He was now too ill to fly up into the cool tall pines, and instead he hobbled over the lawn and got up on an old picnic table behind Yik's aviary where he talked to the residents briefly before he lay down to rest on the sunscorched, peeling planks.

There followed an unforgettably touching scene.

Out of sight, I turned on the tap's inviting water-splash again and immediately Right sailed down and waded in, dipping and bobbing in the charming but private ritual of raptor bathing. By this time we were running the video camera at the window as well as taking slides, for we sensed that something special was about to take place. And we were right, for instead of flying away as usual after a rooftop greeting to the residents, Right followed Left to the picnic table. I should say at once that they had never been on it before, and the

Left and Right beaking playfully on the table

paint of this low and distrusted human furniture was by now griddle-hot under the blazing sun. Right landed lightly and walked a circle around her brother, playfully jumped over him, and stooped beak-to-beak so near that she turned her head upside down to adjust for closeup focus. They rubbed beaks and then she did another amazing thing—she too lay down on the blistering boards and kept him company for over three hours. During that time she fooled around with something in a crack of the tabletop, talked to him softly, and played with him gently; when he looked away she would lean forward slowly to surprise him with a tweak of his neck feathers, and once she got up and walked about, stopping to tug his tail in a teasing way. They took turns having more baths in the full cold pool, returning to lie again and again on their chosen spot, exchanging "yeeap, yeeap"s both with each other and with their foster mother in the aviary nearby. Finally, when I left the window for a minute, they both flew quietly away.

Left was not seen again till his body was found nearby during the spring melt of the following year. But imagine our astonishment when the next day, as sultry and aquiver with heat as the last, Right reappeared alone in the back garden—first to the pool for a brisk bath, and then . . . yes, to the picnic table to lie down exactly where Left had lain before. There she stayed unmoving for two hot and lonely hours, waiting with the patience we find so extraordinary, for the brother who could not come. After this requiem gesture, she never approached the picnic table again.

But while poor Left was ill-fated, Right flourished. She instantly went "wild" again, so that we caught only occasional glimpses of her. Her food-takings dwindled rapidly as she learned to hunt, and presently her visits were down to about twice a week, announced as usual by the familiar "yeeap, yeeap" greetings to her foster mother.

One day, after four weeks of flying, she alerted us with a new call, the thin aerial scream of a full-grown hawk. We ran to see, and to our great pleasure, we found her gliding effortlessly on widespread wings for the first time. Slowly she rose in the sky, sailing leisurely circles over our house and her aviary, calling and calling to those she knew, till the upward spiralling dwindled her to a dot that drifted out of our life.

CHAPTER 7

VULTURES, EAGLES, AND KESTRELS

The Vulture's Secret Weapon

At last after years of anticipation, we received our first injured Turkey Vulture, large, dark, and mysterious. Within hours his deepest inner secret was to be brought to the surface for our enlightenment. Ah, we were so innocent, so unprepared—for the learned authors of the texts we had studied had not had, obviously, our kind of Close Encounter.

Though vultures are classed as birds of prey, they hardly seem so. True, they have a hooked beak and soar as effortlessly as eagles do on a wingspan just as wide, but their thin-skinned legs end in large chickenlike feet, for no clenching talons are needed to dispatch their prey of preference—those defunct, deceased, passé. To find these carcases, these big scavengers not only scan the land from high above with acute eyes but also with sensitive "noses." While the forebrains of most birds have only tiny olfactory glands and therefore can hardly smell at all, each vulture has quite a large one to help him find decayed bodies by scent. Though this ability is a much-debated issue, I have some proof. A friend of ours watched a Turkey Vulture land near a well-filled, tightly tied, intact plastic-weave grain sack that had been recently jettisoned from a passing car. The vulture, highly attracted by its invisible contents, walked round and round it, trying to tear it open; it later proved to be stuffed with fresh-caught catfish!

Our vulture, too, had been attracted by a corpse and had been clipped by a truck as he rose heavily from the highway kill he was attending. The collision broke the last bone of the wing, as well as five of his huge primary flight feathers, limiting him to short hopflights with a dangling wing-tip. Though several people reported his meanderings about the area, he could not be caught till he was so badly starved his natural fear turned to apathy and he no longer tried to fly away.

A Turkey Vulture is an amazing sight close up. From the chocolate-dark wings and body emerge a starkly naked neck and head, incongruously topped with downy infant fuzz over rows of crowded wrinkles. Though the head is modestly gray in the juvenile, it is vivaciously vermilion in the adult, boldly decorated with gleaming ivory bas-relief about the eyes—for sexual attraction?—ending in a hooked, red-and-white beak. The redness of the flesh appears to be vascular, for later this very vulture tore an artery in a claw, causing such shock from blood loss (and probably pain) that his face paled to putty in minutes, leaving only traces of pink in the corrugations.

At first the vulture hulked far back in his sheltered cage, taciturn yet voracious, for any dead thing proved agreeable fare to be nibbled daintily, rabbit-fashion, with rapid tiny mouthfuls, even

A very handsome vulture: each one has a unique set of facial adornments

tails and intestines discarded by the more fastidious hawks. Soon he looked less like a dull heap of sooty feather dusters and more like an intimidating pre-Adamic creature with a glint in his eye that spoke of new spirit within. Fear had come back, and with it, the spirit of self-defense. It seemed to us a good thing, but it boded an unsolicited surprise.

He chose to demonstrate his persuasive security system when the time came for him to be caught and carried off for his operation. As we were aware that parent vultures regurgitate predigested food for their young, we expected alarmed vultures to also regurgitate predigested food to lighten the load and repel the enemy. Further, it seemed reasonable that an established gourmand of decomposing, maggotty, bacteria-infested corpses needs a potent secretion to protect his own health. (This disinfectant ability was neatly proven in 1932 when farmers feared vultures might be spreading such diseases as hog cholera. Laboratory tests showed that this virus was completely destroyed after passing through a vulture's digestive system!) So we knew that his was indeed no ordinary stomach acid. The shock of his secret weapon was the indescribable *foulness* of it.

Cradled limply in Robin's arms, the vulture appeared relaxed and unresisting . . . but he *was* resisting, for all the way he dribbled a warm patter of vomit so fetid that as I crouched to clean it up, my stomach strained to join in. Heave! I swear that twelve years of nursing never uncovered a stench so vile. I scrambled about the floor, hardly able to keep up the mopping and keep down the breakfast, while the vulture continued to effortlessly outpour what appeared to be the full three days' liquified accumulation of far-gone "corpus delecti."

During the rest of his indoor convalescence, we hastened to learn his limits. We begged visitors to view silently on tiptoe at a respectful distance, for though the vulture had acclimatized to our routine to-ing and fro-ing, an occasional visitor would, unfortunately, make him nauseous (and sometimes us also, though we endeavored to control our feelings with better grace than did the vulture).

The broken phalange healed well but his broken primaries sentenced him to a year of flightlessness, which he spent outdoors with Yik and a Red-tailed Hawk. This artificially grouped threesome adapted well to each other; the armed ones raised no foot in threat, and though the vulture was unarmed, he became the Boss and gained choice perching sites by hiss and growl or brusque gesturing with a great dark wing. All bluff. No one ever touched another except when in spring the vulture, doubtless deprived of natural courtship, chose instead to gently preen the Red-tail about the eyes! Perhaps, in the vulture family, it is those ivory decorations that are sensitive to being sensually caressed.

He was released with some ceremony the following summer. With both video and still cameras recording his triumphant flight from bondage to the distant ether, he took three flaps to the nearest fence post, looked back at us, and threw up.

Just an Eagle on My Freezer

She wouldn't fit anywhere else.

Stuffed she was not. Huge, brown, stiff-feathered, 5,650 grams of struggling bulk, two-meter wingspan, feet the size of bread plates, fever-bright brown eyes, feet gray till scrubbed in the basin then chrome yellow, she was. It took three people to overcome her objections to the washing operation. When at last we could properly examine her leghold-trapped toe it was clearly crushed and dying, the whole foot swollen and painful with infection that would have to be banished before the toe could be amputated. We were afraid, for avian foot infections are tenacious and destructive.

We were also afraid of this first Bald Eagle of ours, even though she was less than a year old and very ill. Where in our house-hospital could we keep her? After treating her foot, we were dismayed to find that our best Executive cage fitted like a grass skirt (and seemed as insubstantial). The eagle, however, looked about the storeroom, and like the hawks before her, indicated that the top of one of the chest freezers would be more suitable, so we took her hint, adding a tall, towelled stump on which she made herself right at home. Though we had to forgo the use of the freezer, it worked well at first, for she needed a lot of nursing. She wouldn't drink unless I held the bowl up for her; she ate meat from my hands, looking gravely down on my head in a way that made me feel rather small and alone as I stood close to her twice a day to treat her foot. But I soon found that she was not in the least aggressive—just a Goliath of a sick youngster.

Though she permitted me to approach, touch, and handle her foot, I knew she would draw the line at me trying to open her beak to push pills in, so we bought the largest bait shiners we could get, and served them up as little hors d'oeuvres filled with antibiotic stuffing. She loved them. Bald Eagles eat mostly fish anyway.

I was thoroughly taken aback by her voice the first time she greeted me—a loud "laughing" three-note bray, from upflung head and widely opened mouth. Birds of prey rarely have anything so spontaneous to say to us, certainly nothing sounding so boisterous as this.

A young eagle greets

Treatments went well till the third day when our endangered bird suddenly had an alarming attack of hyperventilation (rapid panting, 110 times a minute). I hurriedly phoned an eagle specialist in the United States. He said she was in a state of respiratory alkalosis (remember the pelican?) and gave instructions for tube-feeding, adding that our eagle was *really* sick, for when healthy there would be no way anyone would be able to cozy up as I had been doing. I was both surprised and skeptical, but as the eagle improved, I realized he was right; on her last two days here I could not approach her at all except in the dark—she was now frightened of me! Meantime, his instructions involved daily eagle-wrestling with Robin and Big Rick (a burly acquaintance who allowed himself to get involved with these mad things occasionally) to give tube-feeds of Ringer's Lactate to balance her electrolytes, and to soak her bad foot in hot water. The bathing turned out to be communal—Rick had to wring out his socks and jeans following the first one, but everyone wore rubber boots after that, and both the eagle's respirations and infection improved rapidly.

By the time her foot was finally ready for surgery, we couldn't wait to see the tail-end of her. She had become wild and unmanageable, careening about—as best one can career about in a converted residential storeroom—even flicking the meter-long fluorescent light tube out of its socket—crashtinklepop—with a flailing wing tip. This lucky incident demonstrated that in this panicky state she was best approached in the dark anyway.

At last all arrangements for her operation were made with the Ontario Veterinary College and she made the long drive to Guelph in the back seat of Rick's battered Volkswagen Beetle. The cramped interior of the now extinct Beetle proved amusingly inappropriate to them both as her giant carton overflowed the back seat, fanfolding Rick onto the dash where he sat grinning with his knees about his ears. Generously he reduced her confines by cutting a large hole in her box to allow her to stick her head out and participate in the passing scene. Her heavy beak hung never far from Rick's neck, except perhaps when at a gas stop, she found the unsuspecting attendant diverting. Though apparently in his time he had weathered many car dogs, cats, a skunk, and even a full-grown goat, his shock on suddenly seeing our eagle peering out the window caused him to spill a puddle of gas and give the wrong change. His explanatory arm-waving alarmed our eagle, who prudently withdrew into the safety of her box till the danger had been left well behind.

In the course of follow-up phone calls with the vets, we learned that almost no infection was found when her major toe was removed, and her recovery had been straightforward. Seven weeks later, she once more breathed down Rick's neck all the way back to Campbell's Bay, Quebec, from whence she had come. There she was welcomed by a small group of government officials, naturalists, and journalists who watched with awe—and perhaps some envy—the impressive sight of the young eagle taking off in flight.

Puck

Late one summer, a rehabilitator sent us a hatch-year male kestrel saying that though the bird was in excellent health, he was probably a human imprint, and would we like to keep him? Responsible rehabilitators do not release irreversible human imprints, but without knowing the bird's history, it could only be suspected, not proven, until the following spring at least. Between prison or freedom, we compromised with parole for Puck to fly freely about the house for the winter; in this way we could observe how he reacted to both people and kestrels.

The word "imprinted" produces much confusion for the public, as it is often wrongly used to mean either "human-imprinted" or "tamed." *Taming* is a conditioning that is man-taught. *Imprinting* is a natural, normal, and necessary process of all higher animals by which their self-identity is stamped into them through the presence of members of their same species who are the mirrors for each baby to see what he is. His biological response might be simplified thus: "So! I sound like that, I look like that, I *am* that; therefore *I must find a mate like that.*" Excepting the myth of wolf-suckled Romulus and Remus, all humans are automatically human imprints for life — even Kipling's Mowgli. A new-hatched kestrel raised by a kestrel automatically becomes a kestrel imprint for life, seeking a kestrel for a mate; but a new-hatched kestrel raised by a human (without seeing any kestrels during the early, vulnerable imprinting period) becomes a human imprint, perhaps for life, seeking a human for a mate.

Imagine this happening with a large bird of prey. The panicky journalistic headline reads KILLER OWL ATTACKS MAN and the poor owl not only gets bad press, but also gets bashed or shot to death. In *King Solomon's Ring* (Methuen University Paperback, 1967), Konrad Lorenz describes two remarkable cases in which birds had become imprinted on a species other than their own:

> A barnyard gosling was the only one to survive an attack of avian tuberculosis. Consequently she grew up in the company of chickens and imprinted to them. "She fell head over heels in love with our handsome Rhode Island cock, inundated him with proposals, jealously prevented him from making love to his hens and remained absolutely insensible to the attentions of the gander."

A white zoo peacock was raised in the warmest room in the Zoo during a period of extra cold weather. "For the rest of his life this unfortunate bird saw only in those huge reptiles the object of his desire." (Pp. 133–34)

The unswerving permanency of these two cases, in retrospect so black and so white, could well have been shaded gray by certain factors that vary the depth of each mental branding—as we found out with an owl called Gonzales whom you will meet later on. Before the time of mate-hunting, the crucial depth is unclear, which brings us back to very tame Puck. At what tender age had he been made an orphan, and what was the duration of this deprivation? Was he just very tame, or was he indeed a human imprint, and if so was this going to be permanent?

Coincidentally we already had a flying human-imprinted raptor indoors, a Long-eared Owl known to us as "Romulus the Irrevocable" whom you will also meet later on. I must tell you, however, that under less unusual conditions, mixing hawks and owls is a bad idea and we well knew it. At first we were concerned that the owl, three times as heavy, might consider the kestrel as prey; in nocturnal mist-netting projects, Long-ears have been known to kill kestrel-sized Saw-whet Owls. Instead, it soon became clear that the kestrel was treating the owl with veiled aggression, following him just above, just behind, with instant parallel flights. Occasionally these dashes had the appearance of incompleted dives, nearly brushing the owl but veering off at the last to land, ready to do it again. Probably it had something to do with an instinctive dislike of owls by hawks, but nothing ever came of it, perhaps because Romulus slept most of the day, leaving Puck to amuse himself.

Whipping incessantly here and there in constant search of diversion, the kestrel liked to play. All sorts of things were tried out. Pens, pebbles, string, papers, dried peas, coins, and feathers were pounced on with pirouettes of pleasure, or struck at with graceful lightning sideways snatches of a surprisingly long leg and nibbled, tested, and often toted away. He particularly enjoyed flying off with pencils which he usually ended up dropping behind the highest shelves of books, along with several scrag-ends of mouse. The vacuum cord was always good for some amusement as it tried feebly to get away from his spirited attack. When the artificial pine Christmas tree was decorated, he spent hours exploring through its branches, looking like a colorful decoration himself. Food was fun. He experimentally tasted many different man-foods including carrots, mushrooms, bits of ice, porridge, toast, cheese, onions, celery, and, accidentally, applesauce, which required a full bath afterward. Constantly swooping about, he scavenged food from the kitchen or boldly whipped delicacies straight off the dining-table. Once he preyed on a hot buttered brussels sprout, mantling protectively over it on the top of the kitchen cabinet where he shredded and ate almost the whole thing, splattering the rest on the wall. He was especially quick to sample all kinds of meat, raw or cooked, and once raised a wail from Lindsay, our youngest son, by suddenly raiding a large slice of smoked beef from his plate!

His regular fare was mouse, of course, and he had been trained to take it from my hand at a wheet of my bosun's whistle, a precaution in case he escaped. He would snatch it off my outstretched palm in flight so swiftly that sometimes I lost a snip of skin with it. But when he was not hungry, his response to the whistle was comic: his wings would twitch in automatic reflex but he stayed put, looking cool and pert, watching me approach with the dinner he did not want. Then he would yawn quickly, ho hum! Or scratch his head. No mouse today.

Puck was very amiable to everyone in the family including the children, but not to strangers unless they looked superficially like one of us. An uncommon-looking visitor, or the sight of me with a towel hastily wrapped around my wet hair, would set him dashing madly about, hitting windows and bouncing repeatedly off the ceiling screaming KLEE KLEE KLEE—the Martians are here! But normally he was so gentle that I could nuzzle him with my nose which he would nibble back in a tickly way, perhaps a risky gesture, as the tomial tooth built in to the upper mandible of falcons is a meat slicer par excellence. But Puck never bit anybody.

Accidentally we discovered, or rather Puck discovered, the one thing that was to make him suddenly aggressive and unpredictable—the live mice downstairs. Several were fully exposed in their clear-topped containers, and Puck was enthralled. I called the whole family to see his behavior. At first we were convulsed by his frantic dancing on the glassy tops, but we stopped laughing when he suddenly flew at us and began reprisal attacks on one scalp after another, raking fiercely with his sharp talons. Could it have been the venting of frustration? Though we quickly installed a bead curtain at the foot of the stairs to prevent re-visits, he learned that if he flew down to the last step, he could squeeze under the beads and once again find himself in the magic room. On one such outlawed occasion he spotted an escapee and darting down, he seized it around the neck with a deadly grip of instant strangulation. Then he went quite mad, wild, unapproachable, mantling violently over what may have been the first live creature he had ever caught.

I tiptoed away and left him with his prize.

■   ■   ■

Kestrels have a large brain for their size — as large as a pigeon that weighs four times their weight. Certainly we got the impression that Puck was "smart," and two things stand out in my mind. One was the first day he watched from his window-perch as I went leaping around the lawn to catch a grasshopper for him; I brought it in the front door, gave him the surprise treat, and went back out for another. This time he understood what I was doing, and when I opened the door, he met me in such an eager rush that he nearly got right outside.

The other demonstration of his intuitiveness occurred several times when I had made the decision to go downstairs to fetch him a mouse. No need to whistle when I went back up, for with nothing said and the mouse concealed in my pocket, he would be waiting for me at the top of the stairs with that particular pre-meal tension in his pose, looking pointedly at each of my hands! Somehow I unconsciously relayed my mousing intentions to him before I went down. Even more surprisingly, I could apparently relay an absence of mousing intentions, for when I went down concentrating on something unrelated (like laundry), Puck was never waiting for my return.

Watching birds at the window proved breathlessly tantalizing for him. If a chickadee or pigeon landed on the sill, he would give a short cry, becoming so frenzied that he could hardly keep still. But his reaction to a full-sized Great Horned Owl fledgling was unexpected. This particular owl was somewhat brassy and liked to stand right on the sill to stare in, centimeters from where Puck liked to perch to look out. The owl, fifteen times his weight and tense with predatory feelings, stared in hungrily at the kestrel who showed no sign of concern at all at the lustful yellow eyes, swinging head, loud whreeping calls, and beak-tasting motions. Puck used to give that *pococurante* yawn and begin to preen.

All his behavior recounted so far was only indicative of tameness, though I was somewhat suspicious of the nose-nuzzle. He gave, however, one other performance that did suggest human imprinting.

Kestrels are hole-nesters, and accordingly, I had provided him with a nest-box which he found unexpectedly exciting. Very often as I went by he would fly quickly in and begin to call a soft attractive rolling phrase which he used only when he was inside his box, only when I passed, and most vigorously when I stopped and paid attention to him. It was the same call kestrels make while mating . . . and it did seem to be an invitation.

On a windy winter day, Puck escaped. As he was flying past the back door someone pulled it open suddenly from outside, sucking him out with a gush of warm house air. Though I whistled myself to an ache as he spiralled higher and higher, smaller and smaller, he never returned despite days of patrolling, calling, and strategically placed mice.

Why, after all, should he trade his newfound kingdom for a mouse?

All Suki's Babies

No one yelled "Timber!" for this tree. But though apparently dead, deep in its heartwood there was a warm pocket of life. As it crashed to earth, four small downy babies were flung out undamaged, so well cushioned were they by their wooden home. They were to be our very first kestrel nestlings, though a steady stream would arrive every spring and summer from then on. Unlike the harrier orphans, however, they could be easily fostered, because we always had on hand a few kestrel parents . . . potential parents, that is, for whether the appointee would accept the duties might be another matter. Our current hope was "Suki," a second-year spinster with a permanent flight disability who, though not a human imprint, had no fear of us. How would she react to instant motherhood?

The experiment took place on a heat-hazed August morning. Taking up the small nest-carton of wobbly headed nestlings, I walked into her aviary and placed it with its hungry motherless load on a sheltered shelf where I could see and hear, unnoticed, from a ground-level window. A minute later I was at my observation post, ready to record. Presently the babies began to make soft chirrupping calls that caused Suki to stiffen with surprise, open her beak, and scream deafeningly for nearly five minutes. Then, while my ears were still ringing, she climbed swiftly up the sloping log to the shelf and hopped down inside the box where I could no longer see, causing me to fidget restlessly.

With her arrival the hunger chorus grew louder, but after a cursory inspection, she jumped out again and looked down at the feeder fixedly, clearly "thinking" about the mouse hindquarters she had left below. Though I had made sure she was fed before I made the vital introduction, she scrambled down and ate again. She then made several "dry runs" among the nestlings without feeding them, despite their fulsome pleas.

Just when I was thinking it was all a failure, I suddenly remembered that the *male* brings all the food to the nest for the first few weeks. Aha, bright light! Says I, I shall be the male. I grabbed a large dead white mouse and rushed outside, first chopping off a few bits so she could choose whole-loaf or sliced. Suki ran away—her flight was dreadfully limited—as I put the offering at the nest and returned to my post: barely had I resumed my cramped stance when she ran rapidly back up to the nest and, without hesitation, seized a slice of mouse and vaulted right in with the crying babies. I gasped with excitement when she soon popped up and whipped a second one in. She must be really feeding them!

Then I lost track and for a long time all I could see was the heaving of her shoulders, indicating the tearing of flesh. Whose flesh? I read too many murder stories . . . the young were almost silent now. Finally I couldn't stand it any longer, and with apologies, I interrupted her again and witnessed a delightful scene.

In the middle of the semicircle of attentive white nestlings stood New Mother: whiskery white fur stuck to her beak, while each nestling had blood on theirs. At their feet rested the festive remains of the partly plucked mouse. At each little throat I could now see the gentle swell of a distending crop, and as I watched, Suki calmly resumed her new nurturing role by tearing off a very small bite and waiting till a nestling leaned forward to take it from her beak. It all looked very organized and peaceful, and thank goodness, they didn't need me.

And so I left her in full trust of her orphaned charges, though I dutifully provided the daily prey and periodically examined the little ones. Incidentally, only the next day—twenty-four hours after they had eagerly fed from these same fingers—they demonstrated a brand-new fear of my hand by backing up and attacking with their tiny talons in true hawk style. As time passed they grew up much wilder than she. If she had no fear of us, how did she communicate fear to them? But that she did.

One month after their arrival, we banded the full-sized flyers who now fed themselves (though with a certain amount of intramural quarrelling), and toward whom Suki now appeared indifferent. We had gone to the trouble of providing live mice on their aviary floor several times a day, thinking this a necessary part of their training. True, Suki did demonstrate the art of bagging and eating several, but later the young kestrels showed us how in the wild they started with simpler prey and all that apprenticeship had been unnecessary.

For their hack, we released them just outside their aviary, in case they still needed the "home ties" of Suki and rooftop rations, but instead, they flew about one hundred meters away into the woods bordering the nearby marsh. For four hours I could hear their distinctive begging calls that in the aviary appeared to mean "Feed me," "Share that with me," or perhaps just "Hungry! Hungry!" As I anxiously panned the trees with my binoculars, one

Suki's baby with broken leg

suddenly flew out from his leafy concealment, swooped down into the long grasses, and snatching up a grasshopper, disappeared back into the same patch of foliage. This triggered a renewed burst of "Hungry! Hungry!" from the others. But being quick to learn, the rest of the novices soon launched themselves to chase grasshoppers of their own. By the end of the day I had even seen them whisk zippy dragonflies from the nodding purple of late summer asters — no mean feat. Back on the branch, crops nearly full, only the most succulent parts would be eaten, the discarded glistening wings twirling blindly to the earth below.

By the time Suki was four years old, she had not only played role model to seventeen fledglings who arrived just old enough to tear up their own food, but she had raised six nestlings by herself. (Two of our kestrel band returns from the central United States were hers. One was a fledgling and one a nestling, both killed by cars five and seventeen months later respectively, and neither had been either mouse-trained or "hacked.") Suki had even accepted a mate one spring and laid several eggs which she did not brood. Given all this experience, it was perturbing when she flatly rejected our most recent mothering demand.

Sated and sleepy, the five latest nestlings huddled in a specially designed new nest-box to await the arrival of their foster mother. Imagine my dismay when four hours later Suki hadn't gone near them, though they were calling very urgently now. I donned light gloves, remembering Puck's mercurial change of mood, and went in to her. She hopped on my proffered hand, allowed herself to be whizzed through the air to the box, dismounted at the door where the hungry babies could be heard pleading within. No reaction. I lifted a section of the nest-box roof to allow her a view of Orphans Irresistible. She turned her back on them, opened her mouth as wide as it would go for an ear-splitting scream in my face, sprang lightly over my head, and vanished into the undergrowth. Having raised six young myself, I was empathetic, but the babies needed her badly, so I stumbled through the rain-soaked boughs till I found her again. We reran the scene five times before I did the unforgivable — I grabbed her. Naturally she dug her talons in and bit me as hard as she could. I stuffed her headfirst into the nest-box anyway and hung some dead mice enticingly over the sill.

Surprisingly, this forceful innoculation "took." Four hours later, when I got up the nerve to peek in, she was Mother again, the mice were gone, five little beaks were bloody, five little crops were full. Sadly,

I did the unforgivable:
I grabbed her

though over the years there followed Suki-substitutes, this was to be her last brood, for she died that winter of pneumonia.

After a month in her care, the five fledglings were banded and released nearby, exploding upward in a heady rush to explore their new panorama. Four dispersed and were never seen here again, but the fifth—perhaps because of Suki—decided to stay.

An Asphalt Death

Though she bled to death, not a drop stained the gravel of the highway shoulder. It had all burst within her body, smashed against the heedless auto steel. Flung aside, she died quickly—just time enough to raise up her furry lower eyelids as birds do when sleep is coming on them.

Every day for nine days after her release near her aviary, Robin and I watched her with increasing familiarity and pleasure. Usually newly released young kestrels get carried away with the exhilarating sensation of freedom and space, flying excitedly on and on till they are very much elsewhere. Her brothers and sisters had dispersed speedily, but she did not; not only did she stay nearby, she even landed on tops of aviaries here and there, though she paid no attention to proffered mice. She was neither tame nor hungry. Apparently just curious.

Quite new in the ways of the world, she was. Inexperienced, her beak and legs clean baby-pinkish still. As kestrels mature, the cere, legs, and feet turn deep yellow with added earthy stains ingrained so that their youth is shown by lack of weathering of their equipment.

On the same day that she flew out of my hand, light glinting on the new aluminum band on her leg, she discovered the highway, and it was there she began to search the ditch for grasshoppers. High on a wire—broad telephone preferred—looking intently down into the grass, her head bobbed repeatedly as she focused on the movement of life below, while her tail flicked up and down as she quickened to the thrill of the hunt.

Our highways (unfortunately) provide a rich feasting ground. In the damp ditches robust weeds give cover for small creatures, their flowers humming with living insects, while car-killed creatures, ranging from dragonflies to maggotty mammals, are a familiar sight. The pebbly gravel of the shoulders, important for digestion, is especially attractive to birds. (One adult kestrel had gulped down twenty-seven choice pebbles—the largest was eight millimeters in diameter. As I held him in my hand I was reminded of a beach; I could hear and feel them grating together in his stomach!)

Occasionally our little kestrel would glide from her favorite perch to hunt further in the small marsh itself. Flying easily, almost lazily, surprisingly large with wings outspread, she would drop lightly into the reedy vegetation onto her marked-down target, pause for a few seconds—perhaps to enjoy the triumphant sensation of dinner in the foot—and then wing her way back to approximately the same spot. What had she caught? With binoculars her privacy is stripped away, and within the round frame we now see her suddenly close up, businesslike on one leg, firmly clutching a very large grasshopper. The imprisoned insect is briefly passed to the beak, not to eat yet, just to . . . feel, to pleasurably assess, as we might pinch a pear before purchase. Satisfied, she snatches it back with the preferred foot (there is evidence that birds of prey are either left- or right-"handed") and holds it up steadily near her face to nibble nibble in a charming parody of homo sapiens licking an ice cream cone. No part is wasted now when she is hungry. Antennae, compound eyes, papery wings, even the sawlike long hind legs are ingested. Later, perhaps, when she is full but cannot resist catching just *one* more, she will eat only the gourmet part—the hind end, where the grasshopper stores sugary metabolic products. (On her postmortem I found five grasshopper remains, quite fresh, three of which were huge abdomens.) Meal complete, she carefully wipes her beak on the wire and takes a brief nap; as I watch, the pale lower lid rises slowly till the lively dark eye is blankly shuttered.

Occasionally she challenges a dragonfly, trying to catch it in mid-flight as it flashes across the highway, or hurtling after it low over the rustling reeds of the small marsh. Excellent eyesight needed here. All of it is on her prey.

On her second day out, bull's-eye! she caught a shrew or mouse in the busy ditch below. Back on another favorite roost, the broad top of a telephone pole, she beaked the small mammal aloft prior to gripping it firmly underfoot and settling into jerky muscular plucking which sent small clumps of fur wafting lightly downward through the becalmed summer air. Like accipiter hawks, falcons prefer to remove fur or feathers first.

Following the act of swallowing, the mouse makes a curtain call as a distinctive "after" bulge under her chin. With the feast safely inside, it can now be lowered piecemeal into the stomach without rushing: a good system where refrigerators are lacking. But what if the prey is too large to stuff all of it into her crop? In our aviaries we find haunch-of-mouse, the skin pulled neatly over the exposed end, stashed into a cool dark corner for another meal. Presumably this thrifty stratagem may be practised in the wild also.

When she wasn't honing her skills by the roadside, fattening for her long southward migration, the little falcon occasionally would launch herself into playful flights of pleasure, intricate with mock dives, twisting swoops, and graceful half-rolls comprising an aerial ballet we loved to watch.

Oh, what a waste . . .

CHAPTER 8

MOORHENS

Semaphore's Secrets

On the evening of June 12, 1984, I received the most astonishing tiny chick to care for—an exotic picture-book creature come alive. On the palm of my hand he stood on strong black legs with huge feet, his fluffy black body weighing only fourteen grams—less than that of a canary. Bright eyes set in extraordinary powder-blue semicircles looked inquiringly at me from beneath a bald orange scalp, his vermilion beak looked like plastic and below it sprouted a splayed-out "beard" of stiff white curls. As I shook my head in disbelief, he looked up and began to semaphore energetically with his naked orange wings-to-be and to peep with a sweet, goldfinchlike call.

Here was a Common Moorhen chick, perhaps two days old, who had been found struggling alone in a small weedy pool; trailing hurriedly with the rest of the brood after his mother, he had stumbled in and got left behind. Though we always try to put babies back quickly, this time there was no way to reintroduce him to his family; I would have to hand-raise him—knowing nothing about the secret life of a moorhen. But at least the fear of human imprinting, the first and most imperative concern for any baby, could be crossed off my worry list, for judging by studies of other precocious marsh birds, he was already safely imprinted to his own kind.

He started his new life on a broad sheltered shelf indoors with a pie-dish pool, a heat lamp, and two Wood Ducklings, who towered over him even though they were only one day old themselves. The ducklings were my only available solution to the next most critical worry—the misery of sudden loneliness, so often responsible for early

An exotic picture-book creature come alive

death in isolated chicks. Though he did find their warm fuzzy company some compensation for his absent siblings, their dissimilar behavior did not really suit him: the Woodies spent most of their time jumping rapidly in and out of the glass "pond," whereas the chick did not like to get wet at all. Once, when accidentally dunked by an exuberant duckling, he collapsed like a soggy black Kleenex and shivered dramatically under the brooder lamp for a long time, crying. He did not pick up food the way they did, and so initially we had to tube-feed him a mushy formula, but thankfully by the second day he had begun timidly pecking tiny morsels from a fingertip, quickly graduating to snatching mouthfuls from a small slag heap of formula on an upturned bottle lid. Ingredients: baby-food beef, strained carrots, hard-boiled egg yolk, pablum, bone meal, and vitamins.

Unfortunately for the little moorhen, his two cat-caught companions both died of their injuries. I knew to the minute when the last one keeled over—2:10 A.M. on June 16—the time when I was awakened by the penetrating distress calls of the forsaken chick. Surprisingly, he retained a good appetite throughout the rest of the day, lunging for proffered minute croquettes of formula, but despite my attentions, his whole-body cries of abandonment (about two every second) were unabated by evening. How would we all get a good night's sleep?

I decided to try a few experiments.

First, I tried the old alarm-clock trick, hoping its loud ticking might provide consolation, and for good measure I covered him with a thick piece of lamb shearling to simulate the softness of his mother's breast. He stopped crying, but wiggled out from under the fur and slept on top of it instead, in perfect peace. But awake, he suffered continuously. All next day I watched him closely, fearing he would die, for he squatted on his hocks a lot and his call-notes became very muted. Still, he ate well, and with the splashing invitation of my finger he ventured into his miniature pool and learned to sip his first drink of water unaided. I spent hours by his side, sketching, photographing, and making note of his every burp and yawn till I came to the conclusion that the clucking clock and I might indeed be of some auxiliary comfort, but he still needed unattainable siblings. In a flash of inspiration I offered him the only replica I had—a circular shaving mirror that I stood beside his woolly bed.

The dawning realization of a newly arrived black chick was charming to watch. His distressful peeping faded as he began to assess the new arrival. Turning casually away, he would stretch an unexpectedly long neck up and up to make himself *very* tall and then peek over his shoulder to see what the Other was doing. Turning face to face, he studied the Other as closely as possible, gently bumping beak to beak. When he felt the new chick was staring at him too boldly, he would drop his eyes and look myopically at his black, rubbery toes instead, for even at his tender age this kind of hard stare made him uncomfortable. His mirror image gripped his attention for about three days, and on June 21 (now double his weight), just as he and his mute playmate began to show signs of dissatisfaction with each other, I surprised him with a big trayful of thickly planted marsh mini-habitat—small ferns, moss, and grasses. Instantly absorbed, he went a notch wilder right off, zipping energetically along narrow trails and vanishing into the undergrowth.

Three days after that, I acquired another small orphan to try out as a companion for him, a baby oriole "nesting" in a coffee-jar lid. Semaphore had been staying quietly hidden in the vegetation during the day, always emerging at bedtime, calling for me to doss him down with fur and lamp. When the new nestling was added, he not only came out of his ferny forest at once (no wonder, the way the oriole was yelling for food), but to my surprise he squatted down as close as possible to the new arrival in an amiable manner, watching intently as the nestling was hand-fed with (his) formula from the end of a food-stick. Unbelievably, he refused to feed himself anymore, but had to be fed off the end of the food-stick too! This harmless regression lasted several days till the oriole needed a more suitable environment, but meanwhile, they spent most of their time snuggled next to each other on a mossy rise overlooking the jungle and received extra mothering from me.

■   ■   ■

Kicking and squeaking in a bag, he weighed in at sixty-four grams on June 29, his eighteenth day, and was clearly ready to progress to another phase: outside. For a gentle introduction he began in a small grassy aviary—the South Ell—whose chief attraction was a lot of insect life and a small concrete pool. Though he never swam in it, he hovered around its shallow edges, searching and sampling, immediately revealing a great fondness for the floating duckweed I had added. He also revealed a hereditary hunter's response to any moving creature. He snapped at the creeping and flying life around him—small beetles, sowbugs, gnats, moths—and from human visitors he quickly learned to expect a squashed mosquito offering after each sound of slap-and-curse (the mosquitoes were irritatingly thick that season). He was quiet and engrossed in the several novelties while I sat on a nearby stump, but the minute I stood up and walked out the aviary door he began crying loudly and running pathetically after me. He was unbearably lonely. When I settled down to write in the house I had to shut the window, for his endless appeals reproached me, and for the next few days I importuned visitors to "baby-sit" with him to give me some peace. Curiously, once any human being was ensconced in the appropriate crouched position (towering over him made him uneasy), Semaphore abandoned him and calmly went off about his business, emitting soft conversational comments. Participation was not needed—only fellowship.

On his twenty-sixth day here, I became aware that though he was not much bigger (now one hundred grams) he seemed bushier, somehow, and on closer look I found real feathers emerging on breast and belly that were pushing the long black natal-down further from his body. Thus newly equipped below-sides, he could now begin wading in deeper water. The little two-meter pond where the bitterns had grown up three years previously seemed ideal, though it was now rampantly overgrown with marsh grass and bur reeds whose submerged convoluted root systems provided niches for aquatic life. Though I was dreadfully afraid of losing him in the rough unrestrained vegetation, it had become obvious that the jumped-up bit of aviary lawn and the small concrete birdbath were kindergarten now. So at sunny noon on July 7, I took courage and carried him to the shallow open end of the water to experience wilder delights.

To my surprise, instead of being agreeably stimulated by the new world before him, he stood nervously long-necked and immobile for several minutes, looking warily about. Just then a bird flying low overhead flung a dark racing shadow over him and pffft! he fired himself silently into the thick reed bed and vanished in an instant. Alarmed, I listened for his usual conversational call-notes, but for once he was completely silent. He wasn't waterproof—he might drown—I'll never find him, I thought in growing panic, peering from ground level into the unyielding thicket, but presently, I felt a wave of relief as a small movement on his part showed me where he was hiding—away in the deep gloomy end of the pool, apparently sinking. I crept hurriedly along the bank till I was opposite him, crouched down, and snatched through the tangling stalks, touching his fuzziness for an instant. And then, nothing. Silence. A few large bubbles slowly rose from the bottom and burst sickeningly on the surface.

I lost my head and jumped in the pool myself, flinging aside the stiff resisting curtain of reeds, tearing up roots, feeling desperately underwater everywhere for his precious body. But after an agonized search as long as forever, I finally gave up. He must be dead in the thick marl-like bottom. Wretched-hearted, mud-slathered, and smarting from thin reed-stem cuts on my hands and arms, I was shambling along the path away from the pool when about ten paces on, I passed a clump of wild mint that emitted a faint peep. "Semaphore?" I whispered unbelievingly, but thinking, only a cricket, you idiot, but I parted the fragrant fronds anyway to peer in and bless you, there stood the endearing little moorhen absolutely clean and dry, and looking (I thought) a little surprised. Of course it was I who was surprised, for I had no idea that he could skitter so rapidly over the surface like an avian jesus bug and end up so far away and so nonchalant. Since then, however, I have seen this lightning defense tactic repeated several times and it always amazes me, contrasting so with his slow heron-stalk of the hunt. I learned the hard way that every fright made him hide, and after he got over every fright, if I sat quietly, he always came back to me!

He quickly became acclimatized at the pond and proficient at both hiding and hunting in the undergrowth. Every few days he had fished out all the natural supplies which I then had to replace: tadpoles, minnows, aquatic larvae, wireworms, slugs, and the entire carpet of duckweed. Only then did he resort to the ever-present mound of formula which he now rated dull stuff, though he always ate all the mealworms I brought.

By July 13, Semaphore, at 160 grams, was mostly feathered and more independent. Yet, except during his preoccupation of a hunt, he continued to mew for my company either when I caught his attention or when he felt he needed it. Unfailingly each evening he called his monotonous peeps extra loudly so that I would please not forget to take him back indoors; this familiar nightly ritual was particularly important, perhaps reflecting a cozy flock reunion under mother moorhen's wings for warmth and safety. As soon as he was plopped on his dear old shelf he would indicate his wish to be under the brooder lamp regardless of the temperature, and would wait expectantly while I reached in to turn it on, causing him to rush under its red glow excitedly, waving his wings with pleasure. From then on, whether left alone or no, he would be perfectly quiet, nibbling formula, sipping from his pie dish, and preening or squatting on his hocks under the rosy warmth until he fell asleep.

By July 15, Semaphore had been with us for thirty-four days, and although he had adjusted surprisingly well to his odd solitary upbringing, I thought he would appreciate the company of a fledgling Green-backed Heron of the same weight who was being briefly housed next door, unbeknownst to him because of a sliding partition. When Semaphore was brought in that evening, I pulled out the partition, expecting him to be shyly delighted, but before I had even succeeded in fully withdrawing it, the moorhen instantly leaped into the Green-backed Heron's half and attacked him fiercely, drawing rasping screams from the wildly flailing innocent who could not get away. As I hastily separated them, I belatedly remembered previous experiences of mutual adult moorhen aggression—but I had not expected it to develop in a juvenile not yet fully feathered!

Semaphore on his thirtieth day with us

By July 20, his thirty-ninth day, the time for release was approaching as Semaphore grew the last of his svelte dark feathers on his head and neck, replacing the bald identification signal-patch, and became wilder, more independent, and, at *last*, quieter. All along I had worried that if after release he vocalized out there as noisily as he did in here, he would be some predator's dinner before long. I made a note on August 6, Day fifty-six, how his silence of self-reliance developed in an unexpected manner, cleverly allowing him to greet related moorhens without jeopardizing their safety. Now when he saw me approaching him at the pool, his welcoming cries gradually transformed into mime; his beak would open and shut with soundless enthusiasm.

Two days later: Release Day. Our lovable moorhen had become a slim brownish-black bird with a short white-lined tail, long neck, and no traces of the gaudy colors of babyhood. We banded and weighed him: 320 grams, heavier than any adults we had received. All that hated handling set off frenzied alarm cries that emanated non-stop from his travelling carton all the way to the release site, but when the upflung lid assured him that he was no longer captive, his plaints died down as he stepped out and eagerly began assessing the real, and perhaps forboding, marsh before him, which made our own little splat seem like a scale model.

I have to admit we were fearful that Semaphore might want to rejoin us for comforting and make us feel guilty when we resolutely turned our backs on him and left him alone. He surprised us all, therefore, by resolutely turning his back on us and swimming silently into the cattails till he was out of sight.

CHAPTER 9

DOVES AND PIGEONS

The Peace of the Dove

One spring, I was asked to give a talk at a local church on "The Dove of Peace." As I am not a churchgoer, nor am I anthropomorphic in my perception of bird behavior, I found it a rather difficult topic to discuss in a manner appropriate to the occasion, which was an evening of prayer, hymns, and discourse whose purpose was not clear to me. I tried to circumvent the mythological and misty-eyed aspects by offering the following:

> Dear ladies, gentlemen, and children:
> When I tried to find references to the "dove of peace," I found instead references to the doves of war. The birds involved were Rock Doves, which are not an exotic species but just our familiar pigeons under a formal name–"Rock" is for their preferred nesting sites in the wild.

Here I opened a box and produced a young pigeon.

> There were 5,000 pigeons enlisted in World War I, and 36,000 in World War II, functioning to deliver messages when travel was dangerous or impossible. The original "G.I. Joe" was a pigeon who became famous for saving an Italian village from being bombed, and he was given the Dicken Medal, a special award for animals, for bravery.

The poor bird had no choice, I thought to myself. Flung in the air in the middle of a crackling war zone, he had to fly to the only "home" he knew. But I went on.

> Pigeons have been used for meat and messages since they were first domesticated in 4500 B.C. The ancient Greeks and Romans used them—even Napoleon's army used them to return the results of the Battle of Waterloo. They were introduced into many countries including Canada in 1606, apparently by the French. In the sixteenth century, a Public Pigeon Postal Service was available to anyone for a fee. We could do with it again, don't you think?

A ripple of amusement swept the assembly, though it probably wasn't proper during a service. The uplifted faces were so receptive!

> Their ability to deliver messages is due to their amazing sense of orientation. Scientists, who have long tried to find out their secret, recently concluded that the birds "home" from as far as 1,600 kilometers by the sun when it is shining, and by the earth's magnetic fields when it is not. Naturally they are very strong fliers as well. The pigeon is one of the swiftest birds of the world and has been timed at 153 kilometers per hour; he can outfly the peregrine falcon on a long-distance flat flight, though he often gets caught and eaten when the peregrine dives on him from above. Frequently, especially in cities, he is the mainstay of the peregrine's diet.

The pigeon in my hands began to flap and struggle, causing the hundred or so white paper doves suspended as mobiles all over the church to sway and twirl gently, so I put him back in the box at my feet. The children in the front row watched alertly.

> Though the city pigeon will eat bread if nothing else is available, their true diet is 98 percent grain and weed seeds. The 2 percent is said to be snails, which I have found on postmortem, and berries, which I have not. However, more interesting than what the pigeon eats is how he eats it, for unique in the bird world, he has a huge crop in his throat in which he can hoard a feast of grain. Once I remember a starved pigeon who gobbled so fast and stored so much corn in his crop in the first five minutes that he became top-heavy, lost his balance, and fell into the bowl

on his head, kicking helplessly, and had to be rescued from this undignified position. Because they eat dry food, they need to drink a lot of water, and they have a speedy way to drink it—they stick their whole beak under water and suck like a horse. Even the baby pigeons feed this way, but they stick their soft little beaks inside the parental one to suck up rich and nourishing "pigeon's milk" while the adult simultaneously pumps it upward from his crop. One result of this system is that the young, who after a good feed look as if they have a . . .

Here I faltered, groping for a new phrase to replace my habitual "forty-inch bust" because I suddenly noticed some still more generous ones present whose owners might not appreciate the reference.

. . . a . . . a pillow stuffed in their chest. Because of this sort of storage tank, the young don't have to be fed very often.

Could perhaps the bright, fixed expressions everywhere be conditioned responses to long sermons?

The other end of the action, however, is annoying to some people. For hundreds of years the Egyptians had the problem solved very sensibly: they built silo-like buildings with many ledges on the inside walls just for the wild pigeons to breed in, then collected the fallen guano, packaged it neatly, and sold it at exorbitant prices as high-class fertilizer.

Some people think pigeons are dirty, but this is not so. When it rains hard, we all run for shelter, but pigeons go out into the open to get as rained-on as possible; to enjoy the most wetness of the downpour they will tilt over onto one side with one wing stuck up as straight as it will go, looking like dumpy gray sailboats about to blow over. The rest of the time they love to bathe every day no matter what the temperature; as they do not migrate, they are very hardy of freezing temperatures. Often in the deep of winter I have chopped a hole in the ice of their pool for the popular pigeon Polar Dip and watched them jostle for the privilege of being first among the tinkling ice chunks; the dominant one sinks blissfully down, every feather raised till he looks like a giant gooseberry. Of course no bath is complete without a maximum of head-swishing, wing-splashing, and chest-dunking. When he finally gives up his place of honor and climbs out, surprise—he is completely dry! This is because his feathers are covered with a fine powder that keeps them waterproofed, and a thin bloom of it will be left on the surface of the water.

Now the last bit. Would this make a stir in the bedrooms of the hamlet?

For those who like to draw moral human parallels from bird behavior, I offer a summary of the courtship and mating of the common pigeon: it is truly "till death us do part." For only then—perhaps—will another mate be sought.

The cock is a perfect husband who never lets love go stale. He daily compliments his spouse on her attractiveness by dancing and bowing before her, sweeping his fanned tail, blowing out his beautiful iridescent neck, and cooing. He gives her gifts of food . . . and makes love to her every day. Even when not actively courting, they loaf together and take turns preening each other around the head, which clearly gives each other pleasure.

Now mated, they go house hunting together for a suitable cavity, but it is the hen who makes the final decision just where the nest is to be. She sits down on the chosen well-sheltered ledge, arranging the "furniture" around her body as she builds the simple nest. Meantime, with a strong air of purposefulness, the cock flies to and from the nest fifty or more times each day, each time bringing a single slim stick which he presents to her to arrange. So Noah's dove must have been a male.

Together or singly, they defend their nest with fearless zeal. Twice I have known a sitting pigeon to be preyed upon and eaten right on the nest rather than expose its precious contents. But brooding the eggs is not the duty of the hen only; all responsibilities for the home chores are consistently divided. The cock unfailingly shares the brooding and feeding of the two babies, and stoutly defends the home from intruders—woe to a strange pigeon entering when it's her turn at home, for though she is smaller, she becomes a tigress. The cock gives her every afternoon off, from about noon till six P.M. or so, though he may get impatient and round her up if she has overstayed her leisure time. Though the babies take up most of their hours, the pigeon pair manages to snatch a few short breaks together between shifts to preen each other and reaffirm their devotion to each other. The pair-bond is so strong that while away from the nest and socializing with other members of the flock, the cock shows no jealousy of the admiring passes made by other males; the hen in turn is entirely complacent of his heavy but harmless flirtations taking place within her view. So at least in the marital sense, I think the dove is indeed a bird of peace!

They were very nice to me afterward, introducing me all around and plying me with sticky buns and tea.

POST HOC   I had thought complacently that the audience had been unusually attentive to my little talk. However, I was rather taken aback when two days later, I met one of the young boys who had been in the church at the time.

"How is your parrot?" said he, sweet as pie.

The Tale of Bumfeathers

Do please accept my apologies for the vulgarity of her name, but honestly if you could have seen her, you would have recognized at once her most outstanding asset.

Our rooftop has been distinguished since the early days of the Ark by a flock of ex-patient pigeons, swelled over the years by drop-in travellers seeking food, rest, and company of their own kind. We enjoy them. There is always some interaction taking place on the small but well-fertilized back lawn where they are fed daily and enjoy the bird pool. For this small service we are amply repaid by being able to observe their private lives. Pigeons are easily identified by plumage, and as our releases are color-banded as well, individuals can often be recaptured for examination or X rays. In this way, we learn about the progress of soft-tissue healing, compensation for disabilities, remodelling of old fractures, and so on in healthy free-living birds. These we cannot learn from other wild species whom we return to their home territories and who are seldom encountered again.

Mostly the pigeons are of Rock Dove stock, but once, drawing stares and questions from our many visitors, there was this flamboyant, stocky little fancy breed, looking somewhat like a bright banty rooster compressed end to end. Her end sported a delectable cloudburst of gray undertail coverts below a short wrenlike tail that pointed not in modesty to the horizon, but gaily skyward to Sirius. She had come in with her leg broken, and after healing, she was released here, where to our amusement she proceeded to reveal a personality as colorful as her plumage.

In order to encourage our ex-patients to stay, we had built a four-unit dovecote with arched entrances fronted with small landings, each coveted flat being won and owned by a strongly bonded breeding pair. A few weeks pre-Bumfeathers, such a bond had been broken after three years of contented union in one of the flats when the female and her babies had been eaten by an infamous bird-killing raccoon. The dispirited widower, "Chequers," had since shown only apathy for any passing females until the day that Bumfeathers stretched out for a lazy sunbath on the roof beside him, causing him to do the classic double take, followed by the Don't-I-Know-You-From-Somewhere? routine . . . and an earthy suggestion that she very properly refused. As with the human race, mere copulation—especially without any courtship—rarely leads to permanency. Nevertheless, she must have made her choice right then, and set out with unrelenting female persistence to make him her mate.

After she had pertly turned him down, he lost interest and went back to his apartment, which is what pigeons *really* fight about, not their spouses. To my amazement, and no doubt his too, she followed him and stuck her head inside his doorway inquiringly. As only a mate is permitted in the nesting cavity, he immediately rapped her hard between the eyes, so she stepped back and stood there some moments, apparently "thinking" about the next gambit in the game. Presently, she turned around, presenting to him the eye-catching adornment that inspired her name, and performed a most unexpected bit of behavior; she backed up right to his entrance and proceeded to lie down on his sunny landing, effectively imprisoning him within. Probably her injured leg was aching; anyway, she rested there a long time. Chequers, a pigeon ever of civil conduct, waited patiently behind the feathery darkness. There was no back door, you see.

After lovely little Bumfeathers repeated this simple ploy for several days, she so filled his thoughts (as well as his doorway) that he came to realize that she was *exactly* what he wanted forever. So he regained his lost vitality and courted her with reawakened enthusiasm—the distended iridescent neck ruff, the low bows and smart turns, the fantailed sweeps with sudden mock rushes, all of course accompanied by reverberating throbs of rolling throaty enticement.

After careful consideration, she graciously accepted his proposal . . .

she moved in . . .

and he got his landing back.

Feminine Tactics

It has been shown that under unusual conditions of stress, birds are sometimes capable of extraordinary responses that appear to go far beyond mere instinct and into the realm of reasoning. Here, in the following story which we witnessed and photographed, is a case of unprecedented behavior in a female pigeon, following a staggering double loss rated as the most stressful an average person has to undergo.

The scene takes place in the dovecote's best flat ("The Penthouse"), a rectangle whose details in plan need describing. Its meter-plus length is divided lengthwise by a slightly less than one-meter interior wall, and its half-a-meter width is fronted with two arched entries, one on each leg of the U. The entrance that luxuriates in an outside landing was regarded by all pigeons as the main door, while the other was only an emergency exit. The first occupants of the penthouse had been hand-raised together by us and became inseparable, bonding early in life and maturing into a strong and devoted pair. In the middle of raising their fifth brood, disaster struck suddenly one night when their eggs were eaten and the cock killed at his nearby roost, while his handsome black mate Tarbrush barely escaped from the raccoon who had oozed through the narrow doorway. Her safe and well-regulated life suddenly shattered, Tarbrush "hung around" outside the dovecote for a few days in evident conflict: though she approached the entrance several times, she just could not bring herself to go over the step, yet the interrupted brooding-drive was strong still. Then decisively, without fanfare, she quickly initiated a mating with the nearest available male (her first born) and the new pair settled at a farm a kilometer away, occasionally returning for social visits.

The empty penthouse was promptly taken over by another strongly bonded pair: a large sturdy male called 4-Stitch and his unusually small spouse, Koo (who months before had been admitted partially defeathered—nearly stark naked, in fact). Regardless of the season they made unflagging love on their roof every day, with predictable results. They were model mates, practised parents, and highly successful homeowners living an idyllic and untroubled life . . . until the return of Tarbrush twenty-one months later.

Now mateless again, Tarbrush mounted an extraordinary single-handed campaign to reinstate herself in her old home. Restlessly she began to haunt the penthouse landing, first merely looking in, then actually walking boldly down the corridor till she was discovered by 4-Stitch and driven out. (Mid-afternoon is every pigeon mother's leisure time and Koo was "off.") This is approximately analogous to a human discovering a stranger stealing the family silver. When several rapid repeats of this move failed to expose any weak points in 4-Stitch's defence, Tarbrush abruptly switched to the entirely different and peculiar tactics of Plan B.

After a quick scout outside, Tarbrush recognized and deliberately offered herself sexually to another cock roost-owner, possibly on the grounds that two fight more strongly than one for their home, and that the home is always chosen not by the male, but by the female. But although she instigated six matings in quick succession, the second cock showed no intention of abandoning his hen and home. She had failed to lead him off. There was no time to waste; driven by displaced hormones, she dropped him like the proverbial hot potato and went back to Plan A with astonishing determination and energy. Once again we noted that she picked the cock's shift.

It seemed that if she could not drive them out, she would wear them out. Invading from the main entrance, in the first twenty minutes she hurried down that corridor thirty-five times, and was duly thrown out thirty-five times by an increasingly harried 4-Stitch, who was trying to brood the two newly hatched babies on the nest just round the U-bend. Each time, the babies grew colder. Now Tarbrush went further still, making it around the bend to the actual nest seven times, each violation precipitating a really furious attack in which she would be captured and dragged by the head feathers bumpity-bump over the hapless young till she was forcibly ejected out the exit doorway. Meantime, Koo, feeding within sight of home, flew back to help, attacking the bigger black pigeon with such dust-raising fierceness that the ruckus attracted the attention of several curious onlookers in the loafing flock. Despite her small stature, Koo finally won, and after shoving her competition bodily over the landing, took over the babies: all these were unprecedented actions for a hen during her "time off."

Now things stood like this. Koo was warming the hatchlings, while 4-Stitch stood on guard just inside his main entrance way. It looked to us as if Tarbrush's last strategy had failed . . . or had it? For now that Koo was brooding tight to the nest, Tarbrush was safe to gear into Plan C, an ingenious third strategy that really was devilish. She began to arrive on the landing, triggering 4-Stitch to rush out and peck her off. After thirteen rapid repeats, she inflamed him into leaving his post entirely to chase her up onto the roof above, out of Koo's sight. Immediately, Tarbrush was transformed from tormentor to siren, sleek and seductive. She was courting him! Round and round she went, making unmistakable, irresistible sexual invitations, luring him to follow her hypnotically decreasing circles till she lay down suddenly, then he was on her back before he could stop and copulation took place. (What an excuse!) Tarbrush then rose and performed a beautiful "Triumph Walk"– my term for the vividly explicit postcoital display reserved for those truly bonded. The devil! I saw now that if she could win him, she would automatically become mistress of the coveted roost. But 4-Stitch's bonding to Koo was too strong to be shaken, and when once again Tarbrush sought to bind him with that potent feminine lure, he hesitated with one foot actually raised to mount her – and instead, he pecked her sharply on the head! And as she continued to tempt him by her submissive position before him, he resolved his ambivalence by seizing her by the feathers of the neck, dragging her relentlessly to the edge of the roof, and whoof! over she went.

That should have been the end, but the truth is that Tarbrush ran them ragged for a whole week embellishing her stratagems with plans D and E before she gave up and left as suddenly as she had come. One of the babies survived. With the strength of their bonding well proven through that stormy session, Koo and 4-Stitch resumed their peaceful life of making love on the roof every day, with more predictable results.

Making love every day

CHAPTER 10

THE OWL FAMILY

Romulus

While Puck was only a suspected deviant, Romulus really *was* a human imprint. She had been taken as a small nestling, raised by a man, and lived in a kitchen for over a year before he passed her on to the Owl Rehabilitation and Research Foundation in Vineland, Ontario, the best of its kind in North America. Nine years there with other Long-ears had not changed her muddled image of herself, so the director, Kay McKeever, gave her to us to be a "public" owl. Rom thrived on people . . . providing they were men. Having been raised by a man, she was now bonded to the male sex, and thereafter viewed the opposite sex as rivals or interlopers; and all children, with their bright colors and high voices, were included as "non-men" for good measure. Though at first she accepted us equally, she soon sought Robin for a partner, gradually showing more and more antipathy toward me and other women. In such disturbed cases as this unfortunate owl, the sex of the human-imprinted bird itself is immaterial, and in fact we had no idea what sex Rom was—it is not officially possible to tell the sex of owls by looking at them, or even by weighing and measuring them (in bird-banding, an owl can only be sexed if it has laid an egg!) and so it was not till her death in her sixteenth year that we found out Rom was female.

She settled down easily to house life. History repeated itself when she chose for her favorite roost a perch on the top of the cabinet over the kitchen stove, where she soon taught us to keep lids on pots to bounce her castings onto the floor instead of into the soup. A bigger hazard was her stashes; for after she had landed lightly on Robin's hand and delicately accepted a gift of mouse, she might only eat half, and like Puck, cache the rest. Unlike Puck, she habitually sought obscure cavitylike depositories, unknown to us and soon forgotten by her. A partly opened drawer, the velvet-lined cutlery box, and my hand-carved leather purse stay in mind.

Rom was like Yik in one way: no fear, no inhibitions. Fury, annoyance, attention, contentment, hunger—we were never in doubt about her inner feelings. Her body signals were emphatic, facial signals even more so. Relaxed, her irises vanished, full black liquid pupils half looking from lazy lids, her head and neck hooded widely by the looseness of those feathers. But the approach of women or children produced a mean tight-feathered look with pinpoint pupils

Romulus reflects her photographers:
left, Rom with a woman; right, Rom with a man

in umbrage-yellow eyes straining out of their sockets, such a profound expression of dislike that we privately called it "the Visitor's Sneer."

Compressed plumage and bugging eyeballs were an inevitable response to ecstatic upper-register comments of onlookers, and in scores of photographs, the sex of each photographer is mirrored on Rom's face! No wonder so many people remarked that she did not look "like the owl in the bird book," and found her disconcerting.

She made those faces at me too. As my stock went down and Robin's went up, he placed a perch on the dining-room buffet close to his chair, where he could give her pleasure. As soon as she heard his approaching footsteps she would begin to mew soft baby sounds which she would continue till several minutes after he had left. Man and owl had many contented tête-à-tête groomings in which owl floated off into a trancelike state while her whiskers and facial disc were caressed, and man was treated by having his nose and bushy eyebrows nibbly-groomed in return. But these honors were for no outsider, emphatically not for me. My advancing hand would be immediately hissed at, bitten, and if not withdrawn smartly, bloodied by punishing talons.

Once we conspired to fool her. Owl was on the buffet, Robin sitting nearby, stroking her face into a dreamy shut-eyed state. Smoothly I glided onto Robin's knee and very slowly slid my hand down his arm till my fingers reached the bird and cautiously took over the nuzzling, which gave me a lovely thrill as I copied the affectionate gestures Rom so enjoyed . . . for about forty seconds. Then her eyes suddenly snapped open—deception!—and jerking her body feathers tightly about her in a persnickety gesture eloquent of spinster-surprised-in-inadequate-attire, she attacked my finger fiercely and banished it from her favors with a flourish. "And never darken my Dior again." No matter how carefully we tried this surrogation, she always quickly sensed the difference, though just how we never did find out.

The little owl was alertly sensitive in other ways too. On the evening that she rode downstairs on Robin's fist, frightening Yik and Sandbanks so badly, Rom had then paid them scant heed, for her attention was wholly absorbed by a tiny sound heard by no one else. Suddenly she dropped onto the floor and lay rigid, wings outspread, dilated eyes staring into space. Alarmed, Robin too dropped onto the floor, but as he gently lifted her up he found the answer: one foot was tightly clenched about a still-quivering mouse. What a demonstration of instinctive reaction, after nine captive years with never a mouse to grab.

On that occasion, just prior to her galvanizing discovery, she had been introduced to another Long-ear and showed no response. Later, when she was in an aviary with a wild, recuperating Long-ear, she showed a negative response, refusing to even share the same branch; as the other owl would land, Rom would bounce off like a tiddlywink.

Her strongest response to the stranger was for another reason altogether, as I found out one dark night when I went out to feed the owls. The Long-ears, like all the other really nocturnal owls, were very active then, and hungry; the whole compound of aviaries was alive with the rustling of landing and takeoff and the whispering of unseen flight. I placed the mice on the aluminum surface of the feeder, but before I even let go the handle there was a harrowing shriek near at hand that made me jump violently. What the hell was that? It tore the air with the piercing savagery of fighting tomcats. Seconds later came the explanation – a light tinny scratching of eager talons on the feeder. Fearless Rom, familiar with my routine, had flung herself instantly over the mice, mantling explosively while shrieking a warning at the other owl, another of many Long-eared Owl calls not mentioned in bird books.

■　　■　　■

These were glimpses of Rom At Home. Now for a glimpse of Rom On Show, for she appeared in public many times, in brisk demand as the centerpiece for lectures, TV talks, and conservation projects. There she was, the living prototype in 3-D. She fluttered her wings, pirouetted on the glove, winked her eyes, nibbled hairy fingers (men), hissed malevolently (women), and even coughed up a bone-packed pellet before surprised spectators. She practically wore herself out being an owl and the crowds loved it all.

Rom loved the crowds too, providing men heavily outnumbered women, and children were neither seen nor heard. Many who came knew little of owls, had never seen a live one before, and wanted to question a persistent "old wives' tale" while their children sought the same answer by running relentless circles around Rom. (How she hated that!) People are still asking it: Can an owl *really* turn its head 360 degrees? (A second question is implied.)

It is puzzling how this head-twizzling myth, irrelevant as it is, appears to have gripped the popular imagination for so long. Probably our ancient fascination with owls is largely due to their eyes with their compelling frontal binocular stare, which we unconsciously equate with our own; further, to see as a man is to think as a man, hence in the "wise owl" myth we also equate our brains. But as we cannot equate their neckless fluidity with our stiff, limited head movements, their cervical pliancy appears all the more magical . . . Forsooth, Sire, this owl can turn its head round and round!

When an owl looks rapidly around and back, the illusion of head-twizzling is produced by the flick of the head swirling the long puffy neck feathers smoothly over the stationary body plumage just a fraction too fast for the unprepared eye to follow. Why do they have this ability to flick their heads back and forth with such ease? Because human eyes roll freely, while owl eyes are fixed immovably in their skulls. To compensate, they have twice as many neck vertebrae, allowing them to rotate their heads nearly four times as far as we can.

While we are so aware of the rotation of an owl's neck, why is it that we don't notice that *all* birds have identical mobility of the head? Familiar birds are just as marvellous. The pigeon, the canary, the robin, all have at least thirteen cervical vertebrae, and not only do they preen down the middle of their backs (and have some binocular vision as well) but unlike owls, they even sleep with their heads tucked under their back feathers. Ah, the disillusionment. An owl looking behind himself is no more wonderful than that of a House Sparrow looking behind him, and no one ever comments on that!

To answer the original question about whether owls can turn their heads in a full circle, a bloodthirsty, superstitious subquestion is implied: *If the owl turns his head 360 degrees will it fall off?*

No. It is humans who are rubberneckers, not owls. Yes, they can turn their heads 360 degrees and here's how they do it. If the rotation starts with the head facing dead front, it will travel 180 degrees to midback. But if the rotation starts (in the anatomically acceptable direction, of course—please!) with his head already at midback, it can certainly describe a full circle to the middle of his back again if he so wishes.

But it will not
      fall
        off.
           ■   ■   ■

Rom lived with us for seven years, enriching our lives and perhaps those who saw her either here, on television, or at public appearances. She was the subject of hundreds of photographs, someone wrote a poem about her, and in her small way she was a byword for the Avian Care and Research Foundation. But in her sixteenth year she became terminally ill with kidney failure, and very sadly we put her down.

Rom's idea of heaven was being surrounded by admiring men. I can empathize with that, and I hope she made it.

A Logging Surprise

Taking advantage of the cool of the May dawn, two hired hands, George and John, drove their battered sedan to the edge of a wood where three of them were on a logging job. Today George was to be the "feller," so armed with his chain saw he disappeared into a cut in the woods while John checked over the big logskidder he would be driving. Presently the engine growled into life and he moved ponderously off along the beaten path after his brother.

About an hour later the monster machine rocked up to the swath of new-felled trees. With swift, practised movements, John chained seven or eight trunks behind the logskidder like a grotesque bouquet and once more set his beast in motion. Along the zigzag ravine the ex-trees slammed, bounced, and recoiled in continuous violence over great rocks and ruts, while on every turn the outside trunks were flung outward with great force, smashing saplings and gashing the earth. In his cab, John was jolted relentlessly, ears padded against the snarling of the engine ahead and the bashing of the logs behind. A marshy area had been crudely bridged by parallel logs over which the weighty trunks thudded forcefully in primitive percussion against those that rolled and mudslurped uneasily beneath. Around another bend and up a hill the engine screamed higher, straining to drag its dead cargo. Finally the logskidder toiled into a sunny pasture, where John dropped the bruised trunks with a reverberant crash, cut the ignition to silence, and headed for a rest in the shade. It was hot and humid, though not yet eight o'clock.

Almost at once the roar of the engine was replaced by the high-pitched scream of a chain saw as the third laborer began to cut up the trunks, starting with an old knotholed beech. Sawdust spurted as length after length rolled away. Knots are dangerous and he concentrated, frowning through the sweat and sawdust plastering his face. Halfway through a big knothole he jerked the saw back in surprise—the cavity was occupied! He reached in and gently scooped out three fuzzy gray bodies that still breathed, eyes kept tightly shut as Screech Owls characteristically do in what appears to be a gesture of denial, as if they might well wish that the past hour of horror had never happened at all.

Greatly concerned, John and George simply quit work at once and brought us the owlets, gently bedded in an old sweater, lined—appropriately—with a cushion of sawdust. Being naturally taciturn, the woodsmen conveyed little of the owlets' dreadful ordeal, but the Screech Owls seemed intact—incredibly, the only evidence I was to find of their tumultous pounding was a short bout of diarrhea. The amorphous gray heap now slept in a peaceful huddle on their bellies, their eyes still firmly shut, so I went off to take an empty Screech Owl's roost-box from an aviary to replace their home in the old beech tree. With George to guide me, I would return them the next day.

As George led me to the site next morning, I began to understand the magnitude of the owlets' hardship. George's laconic comment, "in aways," turned out to be a mud-slithery, ankle-twisting, kilometer-long scramble. I was hung about with binoculars, camera, nest-box, owlets, notebook, hammer and nails, and soon sweaty, mosquito-ridden, and stinking of swamp, I did not make the trip gracefully. When George finally indicated the large partly hollowed beech stump in a clearing, I was further discomfited to see that the nearest remaining tree was a mere sapling about five meters distant. Would the parent owls come to this? No choice. George firmly secured the nest-box about head height, I covered it with leafy branches for shade, we both tucked fuzzy owlets into their new wooden home, and left.

On the hike back, we had to scramble clear to let the logsplitter roar by, dragging a fresh bouquet of tree trunks. Thus I witnessed for myself the great force of the swinging logs ricocheting off hip-high boulders and out of thigh-deep ruts, and I marvelled not only that the owlets had lived, but that they had managed not to be flung out with every bounce.

Next day, equipped with owl food, I stumbled back to the site where I nerved myself to stick my hand inside the low entrance (rather than lift the roof, in case an adult was within) and to my shock, my questing fingers closed over a cold dead limb. Rigid with fear, I tugged . . . and out came an amputated frog's leg! Double relief, as here was proof of parental attendance. The babies were spirited, lively, and protesting.

Ten days later I made a final visit to band them before they began to fly. This time I had to haul them out the top as the box was stuffed with nearly full-sized owls whose vigorous struggles left me a few scars to remember them by. Unnecessary, dear owls. You will be unforgettable.

The parent Screech Owl brought them frogs to eat

Big She

Let me introduce you to the ugly charm of Big She. Because she was only the tenth Great Horned Owl we had handled (the other nine being mild-tempered, critically ill, or dead), she was rather a shock to us. Big and blowsy, the type that makes you feel rather inferior at once, she had a strange elliptical pupil that emphasized her intimidating stare and made her look cross-eyed. Struggling to examine her in a cool professional way, our confidence evaporated as she snapped and hissed and fought. Robin held on manfully while I nervously poked through her feathers to find her problems—seven shotgun holes, which had left one wing limply paralyzed and the foot on the same side without sensation too. We seemed to be arguing with half an owl. We did what we could—pill-pushing, foot-padding, wing-taping—and finally pushed her reluctant mass into our largest available cage for the night.

Each day, with difficulty, we had to recapture her for treatments, and we dreaded it. It was a rotten cage from my point of view (which was level with her large feet) and so constructed that one of us had to climb a small ladder in order to thrust head and shoulders into the arena for the daily dustup that inevitably preceded medical care. In my notes I remarked, "Owl prone to bite and make lunging threats to bite." Few owls before or since have proved so bellicose. Sometimes her furious scuffling made her lose her balance and fall flat on her face, hissing truculently, and we gingerly had to help her up.

It was soon apparent that this jailbird was feeling a lot healthier than she looked, for she spent many night hours noisily scrabbling to scale the walls or bend the bars to escape. Sick owls simply can't be bothered. Her first breakout was discovered by son Nigel on a pre-breakfast dash past the cages to the storeroom freezer, for there in the middle of the passage glowered Big She, crouching on a large bag of powdered milk. She had jimmied open a sliding panel and jumped down, impatient to be doing things owls do at night. Robin and I each took an end of her improvised cushion and hoisted Big She back into her cage, a simple way to avoid the indignity of handling her. (Both her indignity and ours. We were becoming experienced with escapes, and another useful solution we learned was to nudge the raptor on the back of the legs with a sturdy baton, and when it automatically stepped back onto the perch we provided a short ride back to the cage, once again without contact.) She must have found comfort in perching on that milk bag, which served her poor balance better than a perch, for she slept cozily on it the whole day, occasionally working her talons through the now well-aerated plastic.

After four weeks of steady improvement, Big She had gained enough use of her paralyzed limbs to weather outdoors in the space and sunshine of the East Wall Observation Aviary (built along the morning-side of our house, the "Ob" has dining-room, bathroom, and bedroom windows opening into it). It was with mutual relief that we wrestled her hotly protesting form out of that cage for the last time and ungraciously tumbled her into the peaceful reflections of Gonzales and Oido, whom you will meet next. Then we hurried back into the house and popped our heads out the window to watch what would happen next.

Bachelor's Baby

In May, five months before the shooting of Big She, we were presented with our first baby Great Horned Owl, appealing fluffy-gray, innocently trusting and curious, but miserably deafened by two earfuls of squirming maggots. (The reason that fly-maggots are common in the ears and sometimes even under the down of the young of large raptors is because the remains of large corpses on their nests attract flies.) After the treated ears began to heal and his hearing returned, the little owl brightened up. He eagerly swallowed dead mice and crunchy June-bugs whole, and so endearing was he that we found it hard to resist his invitations to play.

Incidentally, those maggots probably saved his life, because a few days previously he had been found and caged by some idlers who fed him deadly hamburger (such meats have no calcium that can be used by birds, and young ones soon get irreversible fractures) and planned to keep him illegally as a pet. However, their amusement soon turned to disgust when maggots and smelly discharge began to ooze into his feathers, so they rang us up—did we want him? Unfortunately their beery, conflicting recollections of his origin quashed any hope of reuniting him with his parents. We would have to raise this now-orphaned owlet, and had no foster parent for him. (These were early times, when we had none; since then, we have been careful to always keep one in stock!) Only later were we to learn the simplicity and success of fostering an orphan straight into a wild Great Horned's nest. So out went an SOS halfway across Ontario to Kay McKeever of the Owl Rehabilitation and Research Foundation for any reasonable parental substitute, and they quickly agreed to send us one "Gonzales," whose life was about to be turned around, if he only knew it.

Meantime, surreptitiously, we entertained the lonely owlet with a lively ostrich-feather duster, whose operator lurked just around the corner, out of sight. This Thing, large and colored like himself, would stalk in stealthily, making him very excited, and suddenly pounce soundlessly on his feet, bringing on a spirited counterattack in which he would triumphantly subdue the Ostrich in battle, afterward often lying down in its comforting feathery fronds to doze and dream, perhaps of his absent mother.

He got, instead, a reluctant father, the elegant, eight-year-old "institutional" Gonzales, who had had the misfortune to be raised illegally as a pet when much younger than our owlet and had become a human imprint. When turned over to Kay McKeever, he had lived a loner's life with other Great Horneds for several years, consistently avoiding their company and only responding to Kay herself. Though he had never tried to court her as a permanently human-imprinted owl would likely do, she felt his antisocial behavior was too abnormal for release. Despite this defect, Gonzales could at least provide the correct parental model that our owlet so badly needed.

Four days after our distress signal, the new owl arrived to take up his duties, and we put him with the baby (whom we nicknamed "Oido," Spanish for "ear") in South One where the bright-eyed orphan immediately marked down this parvenu for his own, and set out after his quarry with puppylike enthusiasm. He snuggled up against him, dogged his footsteps, and grabbed rapidly retreating tail feathers to get a familiar response. The adult appeared confused and irritated by these demands of the owlet, but the built-in male code of tolerance toward the frivolities of both females and young proved unimpaired. In his ambivalence Gonzales would try to get away from Oido, though his ear tufts were flattened in mild annoyance, but when cornered he patiently allowed his feet and chest to be nibbled, and occasionally I saw the little owl tug the great head down to his level to seek out the areas of greatest sensitivity about the beak.

Like shock treatments, these drastic changes in his life began the breakdown of Gonzales' unnatural behavior. From the start he was fearful of humans, hissing and snapping at our approach as normal owls do (and soon Oido followed suit). Further, with the passing weeks Gonzales gradually began to respond to Oido's endless overtures; from a first brief grooming of the smaller face, this expanded into more spontaneous horseplay and togetherness. Six weeks after his arrival, Gonzales began to indicate a sense of territoriality by hooting, and on a night of a full moon I witnessed a memorable vignette: On a high branch perched two silhouettes, so close that they merged almost into one, and as I watched, the bigger half shaped into a whole-body hoot, wild and disturbing, then relaxed, and in the silvery silence came a soft pre-puberty "whreep" from the lesser half. Then the heads met for a prolonged face-grooming session so sensually enjoyed by all owls. I smiled happily in the dark. This adult, long confused about his own identity, was becoming drawn into a warm relationship with an owl—and Oido really had a father.

By July, now that Oido was athletically scrambling and hop-flapping about, he was always near his bachelor father except when Gonzales dozed in the daytime, for life was too exciting for Oido to sleep it away. He played by himself with great intensity on the aviary floor, stalking nervous branches and pouncing on mouse-shaped pinecones. Once, a live mouse that decided to take a shortcut through the aviary amazed and frightened him. He followed it along the ground (at a respectful distance), and when it suddenly turned in his direction, he leaped backward and flapped onto a perch where he teetered, chittering nervously to himself.

The instinct to catch prey needs backup with both practice and parental example to survive the harshness of the first winter, and young Great Horneds maturing in the confines of an aviary sadly lack both. Our then-solution was to keep them over winter for release in the safe warmth of spring when all sorts of prey abound. Until the newly released owls are skilled enough to catch a rabbit or squirrel or mouse, there are frogs and snakes to fill the void; by then their hand-eye (or more accurately foot-eye) coordination has improved from the summer before, and failures of the hunt are safeguarded for a while by a large store of fat. This overwintering practice is now largely disused by us as the early return to natural or wild foster parents is so much better for them.

As the days of Oido's fluffy bloomers and lopsided comically sprouting ear tufts gave way to a more dignified, mature outline, we moved the two owls into the roomier East Ob where they settled into a complaisant unexciting togetherness for the winter. But in early November we gave them a jolt when we dropped in cross-eyed Big She, her feathers awry from her recent handling. I'd say she spiced up their day considerably.

Gonzales took one look and discreetly withdrew to the furthest perch, but this was Oido's first introduction to a foreigner, and he was vastly stimulated. Hooting, circling close above her, he made bold close-up passes, till he landed on the top of a too-slim young cedar bush that promptly bent double and decanted him onto the ground right in front of her. The sudden proximity to this formidable owl made Oido abruptly change to a full-alarm posture, wings outstretched and swinging, screaming his baby call which in this case roughly translated as "Help, I'm only a baby!" This strident shrill Whreep! Whreep! identifies the individual, declares the location, defines the degree of appetite, and inhibits aggression from mature owls of his species. Indeed, the female barely gave his display a glance, being occupied in assessing her surroundings. Rebuffed, Oido produced textbook displacement behavior, pouncing fiercely on a stick and tossing it energetically about, still whreeping.

Though we watched carefully, we saw no trouble among the three owls that day, or any other time. Apart from the natural respect accorded to a hefty newcomer, Gonzales showed no desire to segregate himself as would a human imprint and soon the perch under the eaves became the favorite roosting site for all three, and we were amused to see the smaller shape of Oido flanking the brawny twenty-one hundred grams of Big She who frequently leaned sleepily into the slim fifteen-hundred-gram elegance of Gonzales, squashing him somewhat out of shape in the corner. As there were several other perches from which to choose, Gonzales clearly stayed because he

The Trio: with Oido beside her, Big She would lean sleepily into Gonzales, squashing him somewhat out of shape

liked being part of the snuggled threesome, which became a familiar sight.

Though the days were tranquil, two unexpected visitors began to disturb the February nights. Gonzales, who had been sending off vigorous statements about his territory into the dark and frosty air for some months (aided by Oido's wavery grunting falsetto) had now attracted a pair of wild Great Horned Owls who, according to the current biological interpretation, were challenging his rights in *their* territory. While the wild female occasionally landed on the aviary, calling (once frightening poor Oido sufficiently to convert his splendid male hoot into a Whreep! in midstream), it was her mate who really stirred the pot. He hovered about, hooting boisterously, baiting Gonzales to rapid replies and agitated flights, and conducting a rousing jam session by the quintet each night.

As early April melted the last of the snow, I prepared the final step for the rehabilitation of these three owls. I added a batch of brown mice on the aviary floor, where under the protective, rustling leaf cover they rapidly became wild, burrowing and foraging widely in the darkness of each night, thus providing the owls with at least a little practice in focusing and targeting. Big She, having spent who knows how many seasons hunting for her living, needed no practice for when she struck, she was accurate. This demonstration helped Oido, who aflame with excitement, went crashing through the leaves over and over, terrorizing the mice but usually flying away empty-footed till he got the hang of it.

Meanwhile Gonzales was too occupied trading insults with the opposition to spend much time on mice until in late April, when the wild pair were too busy with their own nesting affairs to heckle him, he suddenly began to concentrate on the ground life and soon became competent, though he had never hunted in his life before.

Night after night, all this was recorded by cold me hanging out the window taping calls, photographing action, and scribbling in the dark as I counted strikes. Day after day I checked and replenished the mouse colony, counted and analyzed pellets, and noted the color of the owls' droppings. (Green coloring was bile, showing that no food had passed through the intestines to use it.) Once a week we weighed the trio to be sure they would be well nourished for their release.

About this time we enjoyed a visit from the McKeevers during which Kay visited her old friend Gonzales to test his response to her. She talked animatedly to him, using her sweetest and most persuasive owl-language of old, but Oido's guardian showed no more response than Big She next to him. This was an invaluable affirmation that his most private views on owls vs humans had indeed been corrected.

In spring, we planned a release party. Not knowing the origins of any of these owls, and hoping they might choose to retain their links, we chose a site in the wilderness of Frontenac Park, and invited some friends and our Flying Angels, to whom this book is dedicated. I had also written about these owls and their "coming out" in my newspaper column, so by the time we reached the sun-warmed shore of a small lake by the woods, a surprising number of strangers had swelled the group just for the pleasure of seeing these big owls emerge from their boxes and fly to liberty . . . though I did hear a child whisper loudly to her parent, "If this is a party, where's the cake?"

A Box for Wowl

It was February and it was raining. For three days the downpour fell steadily over the land, turning depressions into pools, changing snow into sludge, keeping people indoors glumly watching the raindrops streaming down the windows. One face at a window found something more unusual to watch. Not far from his house sprawled a big brown bird with wings outspread, advancing slowly, erratically, through the gelatinous icy mud . . . on her belly. Laboriously she progressed forward on her chest or crabbed along on her side, churning the mire with legs that could not stand; her great wings flapped and dug into the ooze as she struggled away from the road toward the shelter of a distant copse. Perhaps for the watcher she looked like the stuff of nightmares—a sluggardly, crawling mud-coated thing, with compelling yellow eyes disproportionately large in the tightly plastered feathers of her face. Perhaps he simply did not like owls. He delayed four days, phoning just before the thaw turned to freeze-up.

It was incredible to find mud worked right to the skin all over, even in her mouth and one eye. Robin and I hurried her into the bathtub, where with a hand-held showerhead, we rinsed her and rinsed her while the muddy stream that poured off threatened to clog the drain. After much patting and squeezing in an ample towel, she was positioned in the usual carton of pine-needles, upright at last and looking quite relieved. A prolonged blow-dry with a hair-dryer

completed the conversion back to a handsome tricolored Great
Horned, one of the biggest we have had—2,100 grams empty, after
at least four days of no food. These owls are rugged! A lesser owl
would have succumbed to shock, chill, or pneumonia, but our Wowl
was alert and healthy, apart from her brain damage. That too she
would overcome, though it would be five months before she could
leave her box, and a year before she would be released.

At first Wowl stayed in her box all the time, for without the ability
to balance she was quite helpless, unable to rise, preen, or scratch
herself, or to clutch, rip, or even swallow her mice. Wowl calmly
accepted finger-feeding without fuss, and soon she adapted to picking
up chopped mice from a dish. She was a model patient, always found
resting rather primly in her box. But she needed privacy, so we left
her alone as much as possible in her carton on the storeroom floor
with the whole storeroom to herself. However, the one-way window
in the wall let us peep on her uninhibited activities; thus we found
out that when alone, Wowl got busy, hopping out to practise trying
to run and balance on her special astroturf runway. More surprising
still, when wearied from all such unnatural falling and crawling, she
learned to simply fly back into her box.

On a pleasant April day after eight weeks indoors, we promoted
Wowl by settling her box-bed in a sheltered corner of the small grassy
South Ell that had been Semaphore's early playpen. Though she could
now stagger rapidly, when standing and perching she slowly fell over
and thus she could neither rest nor sleep without the support of her
box. By her castings and droppings, we knew she was all over the
aviary during moonlit hours, but each morning she would be
comfortably settled back in it for the day. A dozing but rather fierce-
looking owl overflowing a well-chewed cardboard carton on the grass
is an arresting sight. As the Ell borders a main pathway to other
aviaries, Wowl was sometimes passed by visitors whom she viewed
between sleep-heavy lids, occasionally clacking automatic halfhearted
threats at the more importunate of them.

By late spring Wowl needed more flying space so we promoted
her again, this time to the much larger East Ob which offered
improved gymnastic opportunities, along with another convalescing
Great Horned Owl, a male with a healing ulna. Here, as we had
watched Oido and Gonzales, we could watch Wowl's progress. I put
her battered box on a high shelflike roost, for though she was greatly

improved, she still sagged slowly over if she stood for more than five minutes and so continued to rest in her carton during the day, and no doubt part of the night as well. At first the male dozed on the roost nearby, but after about a week, we saw a new twist: the male began to perch on the side of Wowl's carton while she drowsed in it, and after a few days he got right into "bed" with her! Though it looked mistily romantic, it is more likely that the male simply envied her "nest" and she allowed him to share it. But imagine those big hot bodies in the shimmering June heat, crammed together where there had hardly been room for one.

When at last Wowl could perch long enough to abandon her much-stretched box (though she still showed faint residual signs), we moved both owls to our largest owl aviary—South Two—to overwinter with other occupants. Here the five roosted on a favored basswood branch, always in the same order. This is my spot, that's yours, and the young twerp can stay at the end.

Wowl and friend

One day early next March, Wowl was missing from her accustomed place on that branch, and so I quickly went in to see if something was wrong. I found her in that aviary's roost, once again sitting in her old box. Her problem was hormones. It was spring and it was nesting time, and her mate was waiting for her. We took the hint.

City Owl

Our first encounter with this strong Great Horned Owl came shortly after she had been concussed by a vehicle on February 21, 1986, in the north end of Kingston, just south of the Cataraqui Conservation Area. Though cere-bashed and soaked from trudging through deep wet snow after her collision, she was replete with a recent feast—she weighed 2,050 grams—and her pectoral muscles were plump from good living. As we placed her on her back to examine her, we were disconcerted to see that her belly had a pot, and that pot had a point, the end of a long bone tenting the skin over her greatly distended stomach. On X-ray her abdomen looked like a collector's boneyard. What on earth had she preyed on? Ah, but by next day she would present me with the answer.

Enhanced by the wetness, her plumage stank liberally of skunk, whose trademark can linger for years. As we stretched out her wings to check for wounds or bruises we noted the well-weathered orangy stain sprayed across both her underwings, the last act of a frightened skunk, sometime since the completion of her last moult. Great Horned Owls routinely eat skunks. For these large raptors who have almost no sense of smell, the oily, glandular repellent is ineffectual.

Next morning the owl did indeed present me with the answer: seventy-five grams of recycled cottontail rabbit packed into the biggest casting I had ever seen. The startling out thrust of her belly-bulge was an eighty-millimeter-long leg bone, which along with several other bones, she had simply swallowed whole.

Now wildly restless with restored vitality she was quickly banded #599–04118 and returned to her conservation-area territory, for February is the start of Great Horned Owl nesting in southeastern Ontario and even a day of absence might be detrimental to her success.

Like many other owls, Great Horneds do not migrate. North American band returns or "recoveries" are only about 6 percent of the total Great Horneds banded, so we hardly expected to hear of her again . . . especially so soon. However, on July 2, fourteen weeks later, she was found perambulating grimly over the golf course at Kingston's southwest end, where she probably put several players off their game, for she was in terrible shape. Nearly blind, she staggered along weakly, with caked bloody nostrils, swollen infected feet, and broken, matted plumage. Her still-skunky feathers were badly worn over her wing tips, chest, tail, and upper-toe surfaces in a pattern diagnostic of brain damage (like Wowl's), causing nonsupporting legs. She had been travelling on her chest by "rowing" with her wings and dragging those useless legs for perhaps as much as three weeks. Though kept alive by her store of fat, she now weighed only 1,140 grams.

The most likely cause of her brain damage was a second vehicle collision. Birds do not view vehicles as enemies, nor can they comprehend the speed of approach. I doubt that birds will ever evolve such understanding, especially hungry birds of prey on a hunt when all their senses are fully preoccupied with a nearby meal-to-be.

We worked hard for that owl. With hand-feeding and corticosteroids, and antibiotics and daily foot care, slowly over a two-month period she recovered, another case of the great powers of endurance of this species. She recovered her eyesight (loss of vision is associated not only with brain damage but also with severe malnutrition), her toes gradually healed up, and the skunk spray that had stained her underwings such a surprising shade of orange disappeared feather by feather as she moulted into her new plumage. By the end of August, now weighing a fat 2,110 grams (with no rabbit this time!), we had accomplished what we could, and we released her into the Cataraqui Conservation Area for the second time that year, again wishing her good hunting as she flew away to her familiar woodland haunts along the city's edge.

■   ■   ■

On the night of March 22, 1987, only blocks from where she was first struck by a vehicle, the flying body of a Great Horned Owl thudded heavily off a passing car and rolled over dead. The driver went back to see what he had hit and lifted her body, shocked by the emptiness of the fully dilated pupils in the still-open eyes, impressed by her heavy weight, and made curious by a gleam of metal—the international Fish and Wildlife aluminum band

#599–04118, which I had put on her leg nearly a year before. So for the past seven months, despite the harshness of winter, the big female owl must have indeed had good hunting in the marshes and woodlots bordering Kingston. She survived the guns, eluded the traps, avoided the barbed wire, and dodged the vehicles till that spring night when she met her death, still fat and once again smelling strongly of skunk.

The Raptor Robber

Our owls were being robbed. And they seemed to like it.

In the East Ob three Great Horned Owls — strangers to you — sat on a high perch, overlooking the nightly rip-off activities with complacent interest. It was June, they were fat, and I redressed their losses before they got hungry enough to do something drastic about it . . . such as eating the poacher.

I found out about the break-in unexpectedly. While on a routine evening round of the compound, I noticed a section of their fiberglass aviary skirting had been dug out and loosened, but by whom? Never the owls. As it was then nearly dark, I decided to block it temporarily and searched about for a stake. I was in the very act of thrusting it into the ground when from the other side of the fiberglass there came a most un-owly snuffling sound, followed by a sudden shove at the panel I was still touching. Electrified, I hastily jerked up the stake and stepped smartly back as the panel was pushed open by the nose of a full-grown skunk. He sniffed thoughtfully at the size-eight shoes that hadn't been there before, made a small polite detour around my feet, and cantered off into the darkness. That is what I love about skunks; they mind their own business, and naturally expect others to do the same.

He was perfectly welcome, of course, to dine with our owls if he wished, but it raised several questions. Though skunks feel relatively inviolate, they do have a few enemies, and (after man, of course) the Great Horned Owl is the most deadly one I know, so why did he feel safe in the presence of our owls whom he could surely hear, see, and smell? Perhaps it was the sending and receiving of fine-tuned owl body language about not being in the hunting mood. Of course I immediately wanted to observe this unusual interaction, so while Robin set up a floodlight, I arranged ten white corpses of *Mus*

Musculus "Laboratoryus" on a big stump in full view of the window and we settled down to watch.

Sure enough, about five minutes later, our pulses quickened to the grating creak of bending fiberglass and into the spotlight he came. Advancing confidently to the buffet directly below five pairs of rapt

Kit Chubb

Our owls overlooked the nightly rip-off with interest

eyes, the skunk stood on his hind legs and neatly selecting a mouse, he noisily crunched it up. Then he gripped two more corpses in his jaws and quietly disappeared through his homemade door into the night. His destination could not have been far; probably a den on the hill behind Yik's aviary, for he revisited five more times and though he ate no more himself, he bore away mice each time till the stump was bare, apparently feeding a hungry family about four minutes' trot away. The owls tilted their heads about as they watched all the skunk's movements with deepest attention, but there was never any muscular tension indicating an impulse to leave the perch.

It became a regular evening show. On each of the following nights, we placed mice and eggs on the stump, and promptly at dusk the grating creak announced his otherwise silent arrival. He went straight to the stump, ate one or two mice, and carried away the rest, while the three owls above watched with the concentration of an umpire at a tennis match. Though they never made the slightest move, we did not wish them to either go hungry or eat the skunk, and took the precaution of placing *their* rations up in the roost.

A few evenings later, I spotted him in Yik's aviary scavenging up the scraps the hawks had fastidiously discarded. Like the owls, the hawks merely observed the interloper, though Yik ruffled up a bit, probably because she regarded it as her personal territory. This too became a regular hunting ground through a chipmunk-sized access under the fence where his portly body somehow managed to ooze through. It is amazing how some mammals make their bones flow together liquidly through a small opening. Our cage-comber would flatten himself impossibly under the gap and resurrect (reinflate? rehydrate? replicate?) himself on the other side and be off again.

For some weeks the skunk made himself at home in the two aviaries and on the walkways between, and chance meetings with us were inevitably courteous on both parts. Lindsay once saw me pass down the corridor between the two aviaries with some visitors at dusk; about five meters behind waddled the skunk.

We were generously rewarded one bright morning for our food-sharing with this engaging mammal, as a group of us witnessed a remarkable sight on our front lawn. It was the mother skunk at last, with eight eager young skunks tightly pressed four to a flank, a striking fan of undulating movement as they travelled *en bloc*, with all noses close to hers to learn by scent, all glistening tails streaming wide behind. She briskly led them about her favorite haunts, passing us by as if we were invisible: across the driveway, down to the culvert, around the stone wall, and back past us again. With the tour completed, they wheeled smartly to a silent signal, flowed black-and-white into the dappled woods, and were gone.

A Dreadful Encounter

The tale unfolded when Robin and I drove to Kingston one winter day about 9:30 A.M. The time is important. As we passed a certain man's property where there was an enclosed artificial pond for exotic ducks, we noticed a Great Horned Owl standing on the net roof, looking down at the ducks disporting themselves below. We were surprised, but Robin did not want to stop as it was slippery and there was a heavy van close behind. We decided to check again as we drove home in what we hoped would be about an hour, but we felt uneasy, for it was strange to see a Great Horned so exposed to view in the daytime. I had also noticed the man's car and dog at his new house-under-construction which overlooked the duck pen and we worried in case he too saw the owl. This man had been caught in earlier years pole-trapping owls on tall posts set up by the pen when it had no roof; after being reported to various authorities several times by angry passersby, he finally put netting over the pen, and the posts with their traps vanished from sight.

We were delayed in town and only stopped opposite the pen at 3:30 P.M. The owl was now lying down on the pen roof—dear God, no, please, I must be wrong. I bolted across the highway for a better look that revealed a very familiar sight, a dead owl on his back. Now I understand what is meant by the expression "something inside me snapped," and I, who normally fear large dogs and shrink from any disagreeable encounter however minor, pounded along the highway onto the man's land. Immediately his large dog rushed out and leaped on me, nearly knocking me down and nipping in a very unmannerly way as I ran toward the house.

While I was trying to push the dog off, the man suddenly arrived, smiling and watching the dog shoving me. Through the red haze of my mind, I heard myself asking why there was a dead owl on his duck-pen roof. Still smiling, he said I was wrong, he had thrown the body in the swamp. I countered firmly that I had just seen the dead owl and why had he killed it? Still with that wide smile that never reached his eyes, the man became effusive as he said he hated all big owls and killed at least forty to fifty every year because they killed his pet ducks. Here I interrupted him, pointing out that this owl had killed none as the pen was closed in.

By now we had reached the pen with its two-meter high chain-link fence, and he indicated a very small rip in the polypropelene roof netting, saying that owls did that and got in and killed his expensive pets. As he reached up to take down the body (so I thought), I got the most appalling shock when I realized he was using both hands because the owl was chained up there . . . by a leghold trap. Still with that meaningless smile, he opened the jaws and hurled the body into the snow near my feet, describing with enthusiasm how he had shot it to death. The dog began savaging the owl's body and I spoke in a surge of rage for the first time; get that dog off, I snapped, as I seized the owl. The damned hound continued to molest us both for a few more minutes, till suddenly the man kicked the dog viciously, making it yelp.

All the way back to his gate, I pleaded with my whole being with this man. I offered every argument — better ways to protect the ducks, more humane ways to deter the owls, the usefulness of the resident owls in rodent consumption for both himself and his neighbors, the "vacuum effect" he was creating which constantly drew more owls into the area. Now his fixed, chilling smile seemed to reflect genuine pleasure as he talked rapidly of how he intended to go on killing more owls. I made a last effort and asked if I could at least have the body to aid in our research in owls. I hardly know why I asked this, except I felt that nothing on earth was as important as having that owl in my hands, perhaps just to take it away from him. Contemptuously, he shrugged and turned away.

Rendered speechless with horror and disbelief, overcome with frustration, I stumbled away blindly to the car, cradling the dead owl in my arms. I could do nothing to save hundreds of owls who would continue to die of such blatant brutality — the law was full of loopholes, the authorities incapable and disinterested. I slumped exhausted in the seat as Robin drove away. I was shivering with cold and shock, and appreciated the sensation of warmth beginning to flow into me . . . until I realized with an appalling wrench that I was getting warmth from the dead owl on my knees. Now I understood.

That owl had been kept standing with his smashed foot in the jaws of the leghold trap at least five and a half hours since we had first seen him. Caught in the night, so add at least five more hours of nocturnal agony . . .

That man had allowed him to suffer and had withheld even the oblivion of death till shortly before we stopped.

SEQUEL   I notified the Ministry of Natural Resources who came and viewed the owl. I took photographs of the owl's foot injury. I did a post-mortem and took X rays. I called Neal Jotham, Director, Canadian Federation of Humane Societies, thoroughly knowledgeable on the subject of leghold traps, who told me about a new wording last April (1990) in the law for leg-hold trapping: one must be proven a farmer (tilling) to be allowed to do this.

The MNR queried the Canadian Wildlife Service regarding the possibility of taking away his aviculture permit; they said "we're with you, do what you like." The MNR finally visited him after a week or so and warned him, though this was not his first time being warned for this. His leghold trap was of course no longer in place. No charges were laid.

Questions: How can inspection and pressure be applied to aviculturists in particular? How can pressure be applied to protest the continuing use of these traps? How can this change in the law be made known and enforced?

Pogo: Defeating the Indefatigable

After prolonged cleaning of the eight exit holes that oozed pus and bone chips through the bruise-green underside of his wing, Robin and I let him rest for a few hours. You could be fooled by that complaisant Mona Lisa smile, the illusion of a grin caused by the great width of the mouth; but inwardly the newly admitted Snowy Owl was in a turmoil. After being flung violently out of the sky he had managed to hide for perhaps a week till hunger urged his large pale bulk out to search the autumn umbers and ochers of a nearby field. As there was yet no snow for camouflage, he was seen by another homo sapiens—someone who understood the significance of a walking owl and acted on it. He was to spend a few hours at a veterinary clinic before one of our Angels brought him to us. He was our third

Snowy Owl, foreign to our ways and our latitude, and reputed to die unexpectedly of human-shock early in captivity (it seems to cause something akin to bleeding stress ulcers in the intestine). Though he did indeed endure, he was to become the Number One Problem for seventeen weeks as we struggled to give proper treatment against his lively opposition.

The longest part of his initial care was spent removing the veterinary adhesive tape, layered like heavy casts around both wings, with both wings being then strapped to his body. As most of us have experienced, it is hard to remove it without removing hair (or in this case precious feathers), but by using acetone we slowly dissolved the stickum and peeled it away. Revealed at last, there was nothing wrong with one wing. The other was broken, certainly, but as a nurse, I cannot remember ever seeing both a patient's arms being put in plaster when only one was fractured.

During his first rest period, we were relieved when he hungrily tossed back the five large fresh-killed mice we had heaped for him, carefully feaking his beak clean on the cedar stump on which he stood. Then he did an un-owly thing—he lay belly-down on the wide stump with his head over the edge and looked mournfully at us through his huge buttercup-yellow eyes framed vividly with black-enamelled lids.

These beautiful polar owls, up to twenty-five hundred grams, the largest by weight on the continent, are thought to winter at least south of the latitude of twenty-four hour winter darkness, and many go as far as the southern tip of Lake Michigan. The number of migrants changes greatly though from year to year, mirroring the population swings of their basic prey, the lemming—the northern equivalent of an overblown mouse—fabled for its own periodic "mass suicide." In fact there is truth in the tale, for about every three to six years, depending on the genera, a lemming population buildup exceeds the maximum the vegetation can support, and enormous numbers die off.

It is in such a crucial year that many northern owls go south to hunt the cousin-staple of the lower latitudes, the vole or meadow mouse. When no vole presents itself, the Snowy varies his diet with rats, rabbits, birds, and other species of mice. They have no enemies to fear except man, and ironically they so little fear him that when settling in areas of human habitation they often disregard his presence.

As they concentrate on searching for prey, these day-hunting owls are very vulnerable to cars and guns, and even to birders and photographers, who just by being near, frighten off the prey.

In captivity these birds are extraordinarily sensitive and highly stressed by the strange and menacing surroundings, and it is often extremely difficult, occasionally even impossible, to start them eating voluntarily. As they need a lot of prey daily, our Snowy's uncritical acceptance of our food offering was one big problem solved; for once they begin to eat, they will continue. But though we had no hint of it at this time, our owl was going to provide us with other headaches.

After the much-needed rest, we carried the Snowy back to the treatment room to finish the job. The routine removal of dirty feathers driven in with the force of each pellet was made more difficult by having to burrow through the thick Arctic insulation. Unless the pellets are visible, they are left alone, for only if they are swallowed can they cause lead poisoning. As Robin held the Snowy's powerfully muscled legs firmly, I tweaked out the last wet tuft, rinsed the wounds, put a light cast on his wing, and poked an antibiotic to the back of his throat. Our eyes met, reflecting the silent question: Would this owl ever be able to fly again? The X-ray showed that the metacarpal bone was shattered into a dozen fragments. In theory our latticework thermoplastic cast (exactly like the pelican's) was the perfect support to allow the putrefying wounds to be attended daily. But in practice we had to contend with the reviving strong-willed personality of this young Snowy, and as each day he felt so much better, the treatment sessions got so much worse.

He tolerated nothing. Tapes were torn off, casts flung away, splints-over-casts were destroyed overnight, and each new morning found him standing defiantly amid finely shredded medical debris. Storm warnings were all too evident each time we approached his large wood-dowelled door, for he would begin to leap up and down pogo-stick fashion to intimidate us (which he did quite successfully). When finally captured by force, he would struggle and fight for his very life, fiercely clenching and unclenching his killing talons. These were nerve-wracking times for all of us. (Once when a lady visitor asked us the maddeningly irrelevant question, "What do you call him?" Robin's brisk reply was: "SIR!") Most birds of prey are quite passive while being examined and treated, and like the pelican, can be trusted to leave their supports alone.

A "sweater" was a device of Kay McKeever's that we had occasionally been driven to use in those early years to prevent an owl from worrying at a wing that feels "wrong" to him, though the style soon passed out of fashion with us, as it created more problems than it solved. But after a fortnight of failing to strap a splint on longer than twelve hours (score: Chubbs 0, Owl 14), we were desperate and tried this body-stocking thing that was taped closed both at the neck and at the base of his tail but which left his cloaca, legs, and good wing free. Released back into his cage, Pogo looked hilarious in his fisherman's turtleneck. Now surely the cast could not be disturbed, we said to each other, eyeing our handiwork with some pride. But did the Mona Lisa smile look a little pursed around the edges?

During the night we sleepily registered ominous muffled big-body bumping about next door, and sure enough the sweater, though still dangling limply from his neck, was an unrecognizable mass of useless tatters by daylight.

Kat Chubb

Pogo's Mona Lisa smile

But finally we found a way to defeat the Indefatigable. Pogo's strong beak just couldn't get a grip on a sheath made of tough, slippery old X-ray film, which protected the precious cast for two straight weeks; when we re X-rayed the wing we found all the chips and fragments of the bone at last stoutly united. But there could still be tendon, muscle, or nerve damage present. Would he really be able to fly on it?

At last the day approached to try the restless Snowy outside. It was now two months since his arrival (ridiculous! It should have been healed in three weeks) and wing exercise was much needed. Actually it was the owl's decision, not mine, for I had just inspected the January weather and thought it too cold for the transfer, when I discovered Pogo unexpectedly prowling around the storeroom, very excited. He had just opened his sliding door and "escaped." As I approached him, my eyes lowered to avoid a stare, I noticed that his massive furry foot was clutching a small handmade pottery vessel—ah, you jailer, one more step and I'll drop the thing—so I backed quietly out of the room to give him time to calm down. Later when he was empty-footed, I lassoed him with a blanket on the slippery top of one of our chest freezers and outside he went, trying to kill the blanket all the way.

I put him in South One, where he could get about easily if his flight was limited, and where I could watch from the basement window. There, with camera at the ready, I spent four uncomfortable hours waiting for him to try his wings. Meanwhile the owl, blissfully at home in the swirling snow and whipping wind, stood rooted, watching all moving things with rapt intensity before he suddenly opened his wings and flew lightly, effortlessly, out of sight. Triggered with stiff excited fingers, the camera recorded the triumph of the huge white wingspan filling the viewfinder, and even though the photograph is out of focus you can make out that enigmatic smile. Perhaps due to the unusual angle, it looks more like a grin of delight.

A Snowy Flies Home—in a Hercules

A falconer, employed at the Trenton Air Force Base to keep birds off the runways, was sitting outside eating his lunch, watching a large Snowy Owl eat hers. The owl had swooped on a small bird and carried it up to a favorite high perch to enjoy. A few puffs of downy feathers drifted lightly away, the owl swallowed, the meal was finished. Fastidiously, as all birds do after eating, she leaned down to clean her beak on a high-voltage wire, but unfortunately she was grounded by the pole on which she stood. The falconer leaped to his feet and ran to find her as she fell, unconscious, and drove her to us.

The limp, somewhat battered black-barred owl was reviving when she arrived. There was a burn up her nostril, she was partly paralyzed, and heaven knows what was scrambled in her poor brain; in psychiatric patients, electric shock treatments produce temporary amnesia. But she would recover surprisingly quickly.

The puzzling question was why was she in Trenton in mid-July? At our latitude, healthy Snowies leave for their Arctic home from February to April. The answer, or part of the answer, was on her leg, and when the band number was processed it showed that she had been released from captivity in Ingersoll (near the north end of Lake Erie) in May, rather late for migration. Instead, she wandered along the coastline till she found the airport, whose large expanses of flat treelessness, perhaps reminiscent of the open tundra, frequently attract Snowies.

By early August she was healthy and ready for release, but she did not belong here as migrating Snowies do not arrive in our latitude till November or later. The photoperiod would be wrong, and wouldn't it be risky for a large white owl during the September hunting season? We were equally reluctant to keep her longer than need be, for further captivity might be fatal to such a highly stressed species who had already had her share of bad luck. When a friendly major in the Air Force made special arrangements (which took six weeks) for a flight to Frobisher Bay where the owl would be met by the RCMP, we were extremely grateful, and said so.

The owl said nothing, but her relief must have been enormous when, after being packed up like a piece of rare china and vibrated noisily for five hours in an old Hercules military transport, the box flaps were at last ripped open. She sprang past the grinning faces of the RCMP officers and crew, flying with awesome big-owl strength to become a pulsating white dot over her dark distant tundra. Good hunting, owl, and feak on the pole next time!

Later I received an enthusiastic letter from the Inspector of the RCMP detachment at Frobisher Bay, giving details and a dozen photographs of the unusual release that clearly cheered up a cold blustery day for them all.

CHAPTER 11

WOODPECKERS

Raising Baby Pileateds

It is hard to imagine how living creatures can survive a crashing fourteen-meter fall and sustain only a few bruises, but mind you, like Suki's orphans and the baby Screech Owls, the nest tree was felled with them *in* it. The ground shook in protest as branches crackled and the ugly chain-saw whine ground to a stop. Deafening silence . . . broken by an eyebrow-raising new sound – the "zzzzt zzzzt zzzzt" chorus of two frightened Pileated Woodpecker nestlings still deep in their nest-hole. Technically they were not yet "orphans," for both parents were certainly flying anxiously about, but the thought of making up and hanging high a giant substitute containing a nest-cavity about two hundred millimeters wide and seven hundred millimeters deep was beyond us. Sometimes it takes a pair a month to dig that hole! Besides, raising them would be the opportunity of a lifetime. Pileateds are not only the biggest woodpeckers in North America, but uncommon, as their nesting is completely dependent on undisturbed areas of mature timber with large diameter trees not far from water, requisites that are rapidly decreasing.

How old were they? Visitors regularly and earnestly ask this irritating question, which is so difficult to answer without the hatch day being known. This is a direct reflection of our automatic Western social response to seeing someone's baby whose hatch day is *very* well known. Ironically, without the questioner (or even the questionee) being thoroughly familiar with the full breeding cycle of the particular bird, the answer is meaningless, as there is so much variation. However, we anticipated the query and looked up our bird books.

Judging by the nestlings' eyes, which were open, and their flight feathers, which were "in blood," we guessed that they might have been about nine days old and could be expected to be in their nest for another thirteen days.

The babies were lively and enchanting to observe. Their broad, soft, half-length beaks hinged with thick yellowish flanges rhythmically opened and closed as they issued continuous contact-calls. A lot of naked skin showed down their backs between the tracts of black sprouting sheaths (baby woodpeckers have no fuzzy down stage, but start growing real feathers at once) and when they prepared for sleep, each snugged his beak incongruously down the bare tract under phantom feathers. As they dreamed, their dancing rapid eye movements behind shuttered lids were joined by their tongues working busily in subconscious feasting. All bird tongues have a central bone joined to two thin flexible bony runners flattened between the skin and the base of the skull, and as the tongues of woodpeckers are extremely long, the two runners curve over the top of the skull, ending at one of the nostrils (they have to be stored somewhere!). Dreaming of food caused the tongue-runners to wiggle and twitch comically under the thin translucent scalps, clearly visible through the spiky brushcuts of poppy-scarlet. These sensitive tongues, so much longer than their beaks, later drummed and tested everything around them. When I let one "taste" my cheek, the sensation was intriguing — a vibrating rubbery tattoo of investigation.

As soon as they arrived, the other end produced one of the biggest encased droppings I've ever seen, roughly the size of an eight-centimeter eraser and the shape of an elongated light bulb. It weighed 8 grams, or 3.3 percent of the nestling Pileated's 240 grams, which so impressed me that I immediately photographed it. Comparatively, a fifteen-kilogram human baby would be producing a half-kilogram offering every thirty minutes!

Although we had raised over thirty bird species, these little charmers were new to us, but they grew apace on the following experimental diet: baby-food beef; hard-boiled egg yolk; crushed bone-meal tablets; Nutrical (a high-cal multivitamin supplement for dogs); finely chopped prunes, apple, peanuts, and hulled sunflower seeds; and good old pablum. All this was mixed into a manageable paste which they gobbled and sucked enthusiastically from the end of a finger. After the second week we substituted canned dog food in place of the baby food (dog food is quite a reasonable short-term food substitute for some birds). To supplement the formula with as much natural food as possible, we would turn on the outside lights after dark and grab crunchy June bugs, which proved to be acceptable only after each unfortunate beetle had first been slit lengthwise, for the Pileateds would make quite a fuss about spitting it back if it tickled within.

As they grew older, we noted another unusual point about feeding; either they really *loved* having something long shoved down their throats or else they did require more moisture than other nestlings, for they never seemed satisfied until they had had sometimes up to four cc of water, one cc at a time, from a five-cc plastic eyedropper after each feed. Their all-insect diet in the wild would have provided more fluid.

For the first seven days our red-headed delights spent their nestling life in the basement in a large, lidded carton tree-substitute with an entrance hole cut in it. Being unable to see inside to locate eager mouths, I also cut the box in half horizontally on three sides to hinge the top back, enabling me to play my role of Parent Provider and Fecal-Sac Remover more adeptly. At the very beginning, though, before we learned the secret trigger to make them gape properly, we had an awful time getting them to feed. I tried thick mixes and thin mixes, tapping the box and touching them on the side of the beak, attempting parental-arrival noises and so on, but they remained uniformly indifferent to all endeavors, and we did not want to resort to force feeding them.

After a long, frustrating bout of varied but fruitless techniques, I sagged wearily against the wall, accidentally brushing the nearby light switch off. The sudden darkness sparked a frantically screaming chorus of wide-mouthed "zzzzts" and my loaded finger, still in the hole, was seized and powerfully sucked down a hot throbbing throat till it was so clean it was nearly dry—a most peculiar but gratifying sensation. Once revealed, the secret was so simple: being hole-nesters, the arrival of a food-bearing parent blocked out the light at the entrance! We had a great deal of fun demonstrating this trigger principle to marvelling visitors till the woodpeckers came of age and fledged from their "tree."

The initiation rites of fledging took place at the end of their first week with us, when they stopped sleeping most of the day in a casual tangle on the nest floor and began instead to cling cautiously to a branch placed within. This was followed soon by daring to pop out the entrance to sample Life outside. At this stage they were moved into a roomy unit (made by withdrawing three dividers from the intensive-care cages), furnished with many sturdy-barked trunks and branches on which they climbed eagerly about, sometimes falling off in their hurry, tasting and feeling everything with those incredible tongues. Chipping off bark flakes with accurately angled blows — so professional! — proved to be a built-in ability. Now no longer in the confines of the box, the temporary color-bands we had placed on their legs allowed us to distinguish them as we watched them quietly through the one-way mirror in the wall.

Presently Yellow found the pie-dish pool and learned to drink. While I was splashing my finger repeatedly in the water dish, this first aquatic invitation produced an unexpected reaction from Green that looked alarmingly like acute abdominal spasms as he rolled about, quivering convulsively on the pine-needle floor; but he was only making instinctive bathing movements to accompany the water music!

Swiftly their climbing became surer and we were impressed by the sharpness of their claws, literally, when they began to fly out of the cage to land thud on our legs and barber-pole rapidly up the trunk, tapping and tasting all the way. Inspection, not affection. As it often turns out when raising two or more of the same species together without a foster parent, while they were not afraid of us, they were not deeply attached to us either.

Two weeks after admission they showed signs of restless discontent with their indoor confines and so were ushered out the dining-room window into the so-useful East Ob aviary where we watched, sketched, and photographed their antics closely. After some dizzy initial hours of exploration, sunbathing, and so on, the time came for their first outdoor feed. But though they whickered anxiously in response to our signals, they did not come back to us at the window as we had hoped: rather naturally, they expected us to fly to them. So on the Mountain-to-Mahomet principle we put up two ladders at their favorite resting spots and climbed up to feed them there till they learned that curb service at the window was much faster. This took about a day and a half. Partly due to uncertainty, their reticence appeared to be also partly due to lack of pilot practice; though they could easily fly the straight eleven meters of the aviary, this aerial tobogganing showed little control. Despite strong intention-movements of banking, their impetus carried them whizzing straight by.

Right from the day of arrival, it was possible to tell them apart by minor mannerisms, though they looked and weighed exactly the same. Green, for instance, always ate much more than Yellow, whose refusal of further food was expressed by curious swinging avoidance-feints of the head accompanied by vigorous beak-stropping, while fully stuffed Green merely backed slightly out of dropper range. As they grew up, a certain antagonism revealed itself between these two males: Green showed dominance at the top of the favorite diagonally placed tree trunk, driving Yellow off (or round under the trunk) with sharp pecks, especially at dusk when a choice solitary roosting site for the night was evidently important. I believe that most adult woodpeckers have a preferred hole in which to sleep.

Once fledged, their "zzzzt-zzzzt" feeding responses faded gradually, but they kept up constant "conversation" during daylight hours. With the window closed, it was amusing to see the lower jaws silently opening and shutting continually. But when they wanted us to hear them, we certainly heard them. First thing every morning their hunger cries woke us (and perhaps some neighbors as well) for these were loud ringing "kaaak kaak kaak kaak" calls, very flickerlike. As soon as I opened the window they would launch together from their perch two meters away and go sailing past in frustrated tandem, landing at the other end of the aviary, and rushing back, managing this time, to target to me. I would then feed them over and over till the gratified creatures were murmuring soft little phrases that now ended on a pleasant interrogative note, something like "ma ma ma ma maa? ma ma ma ma maa?" Once, Green jumped onto my jacket and hopped around to hang from my hood as I made breakfast while Yellow merely crouched on the sun-flooded windowsill log echoing his brother's sounds of stomach satisfaction. This familiarity was fearlessness, not tameness in the pet sense, for though they needed our help they hated to be handled, and we spared them this indignity as much as possible.

They were getting big now, and soon they would have their temporary color-bands exchanged for official numbered ones, the high hatch door would be opened for their final stage, and just as the fledgling hawks Right and Left had done, they would learn about natural free-flying life while returning regularly for food till they were

*They expected us
to fly to them*

independent. This woodpecker-hack-from-home had worked perfectly with young flickers.

Though Green and Yellow were only moved by cupboard-love for us, I have to admit we were moonstruck over their dual charms. They were constantly on my mind; gnawing worry, anxious plan, burst of delight. It is not considered "professional" for rehabilitators to get attached to their charges, is it? But this time, we lost our detachment. Quite simply, we loved them dearly.

On the morning of their seventh day outdoors, I awoke later than usual to the leaden darkness of heavy rain, and quickly hurried to feed them—they must be very hungry by now. But as I slid open the windowpane, a dreadful fear gripped me: no calls. No eager Pileateds. The only sound was the drumming of the downpour. I couldn't see them anywhere. Could they be too wet to fly? Frantically I rushed out and flung myself through the tall ostrich ferns that jungled their aviary, heedless of drenching, tearing apart the trembling fronds till I found Green . . . or what was left of him, . . . a mute semicircle of black-and-white feathers flattened on the soaking earth beside his leg band. Above, clinging in a death-grip to the chain-link hung a single dismembered, yellow-banded leg.

Kneeling alone in the rain, I wept for them.

■   ■   ■

There was no sign of Yellow's body. He must have been dragged away by the powerful raccoon who had torn apart a panel of fiberglass skirting and then climbed easily up the sloping tree trunk (provided, ironically, just for them) to take the sleeping woodpeckers.

R.I.P. little ones. You were wonderful to know.

CHAPTER 12

PASSERINES

Games with a Raven

No wonder this bird has impressed poets and populations throughout history. The damned thing can *think*.

When most of our patients are wild and frightened stiff of us, having a bouncy, fearless, fun-seeking go-go raven is a series of astonishments. The raven is rarely seen in the Kingston area, and this one, from New Brunswick, was only the second we had seen close up. Imagine a glossy black bird the size of a large hawk that springs toward you in erratic doglike leaps of eagerness when you open the gate, which you can leave open if you like. He doesn't give a fig about escaping, he wants to play with you as well as to enjoy whatever treats you may have brought to fill his innards.

He attends to the more pressing need first, but quite delicately, even though it is fourteen hours since he last ate. Neatly he takes a small taste of each item in the dish and then mentally plans its disposal: to swallow, or to cache? His instinct is to plan for tomorrow before gratifying his needs of today, so he carefully selects the most suitable food and tosses back a beakful into his chin-crop for transportation to a site of his choice, where he tips it out and expertly pulls grass and plants over it. I look away for a minute and then back and know I have lost the location completely, but he won't forget where it is.

Returning to his meal, he decides midway through that perhaps it will be more pleasant to dine on the top of his favorite tall stump, and does his best to take the entire dish and contents up there "on the deck," so to speak. He fails only because one wing is permanently handicapped after an automobile accident that badly broke his humerus. But he manages quite well when it is partly empty, and once up there he finishes off the contents with deliberate satisfaction and then picking up the empty dish in his big beak, he flings it into space, intently following its clattering descent on the slope.

Now he jumps down and comes back to me, standing at my feet and looking up for further amusements, his dark eyes kindled with expectation. If I don't produce, he may well start in on my shoes and slacks. Pinch, hammer, tug. That is a heavy, powerful beak, Fourteen-Tools-in-One, of which I know that one is a vise-grip, because a wilder raven once seized my tea finger, leaving it without feeling (after the initial agony) for about two weeks. This bird's beak is also an all-purpose catcher of items whizzing unwarily by; a flying dead mouse, flung by me, is acknowledged with a short "grock" just before it is neatly fielded. I play this game with him often, because I am bedazzled by his effortless accuracy and the fact that he always finds time to make a short comment about its arrival before leaning out to capture it. His coordination and precision are truly startling, but the most disconcerting part of the game is a suspicion that he is humoring me.

He looked up
for further amusements,
his dark eyes kindled
in expectation

So far I've only mentioned edibles, but the raven carefully examines all sorts of nonfood items to establish their entertainment value: pencils, clothespegs, the paper on which I'm writing, the book which I am reading. On these cool sunny fall days I sometimes sprawl in our plastic dome greenhouse after lunch (the same dome in which the baby bitterns began their new life) and the raven, lonely in the uninspiring enclosure surrounding the dome, is drawn irresistibly to extract amusement from my drowsing company. When he gets bored with hauling tomatoes off their vines and trundling them outside, he starts in on me, and I soon find out that feigning dead just gets his dander up. Revival techniques that prove effective include a concentrated attempt to remove a leg freckle and a rousing hoarse scream just under my nose, blasting me with his pink breath.

In a burst of irritation I finally shoo him out and shut the door, trying to recapture my fleeting siesta, but he soon proves equal to this challenge by walking around the dome to the point nearest to me and thudding rhythmically on the polyvinyl until a hole appears big enough for him to squeeze back in. Confound him. After I block this off, though, I use my superior intelligence to win my solitude by opening the door invitingly but placing a bicycle inner tube on the ground across the doorway. He shows great fear of this Thing and refuses to step over it; large snakelike objects strike fear in many creatures. Only a matter of time, though, before he learns how dead it is, and though he shudders deliciously each time he tentatively compresses its rubbery surface, he finally overcomes the threatening obstruction by finding a way to detour it. We are back to the tomatoes and leg freckles again.

He doesn't get along with other patients in the spa, though. He pesters them persistently, till I have to remove the visitor lest some much-needed feathers be pulled out. Deafness is apparent when I tell him sharply to cease and desist, for he is far too absorbed in his teasing tactics. But he really gets his comeuppance one fine day from a large powerful Herring Gull that I bring to bathe in the raven's big pool. The gull floats off gently, immobile, with wings partly spread, unintentionally offering the fun-loving raven on the bank an irresistible wing tip to yank on. The gull turns a pale eye on the raven, snaps very suddenly, and clack! there is raven's beak imprisoned inside the gull's. The gull now gives a sharp jerk and the big black bird, despite his heavier weight, is hauled headfirst into the pool, sputtering.

After that, he leaves Herring Gulls alone.

The sight of heavy gloves greatly upsets him as they represent being handled, an indignity he hotly resents. When I go back into the enclosure to fetch the gull from its daily bath, I am amazed when the raven breaks off his friendly overtures and leaps away from me, growling. He then snatches at my hands aggressively, yanking and tearing the leather fingers till he gets one glove off, and proceeds to punish it to death and then hide the battered corpse.

The vocabulary of the raven is remarkable in its variety and use of phonetic variations, sounding like a foreign language that uses a lot of vowel sounds. Some books describe raven talk as gargling, hoarse, or gutteral, but I think the key is the expressive delivery. His gossipy warbling monologues, delivered to himself (I eavesdropped), are immensely comical to overhear, and his language is full of verve and emphasis and heavily laced with italics.

His sleek-feathered body, however, has little expression. Upon suddenly catching sight of Romulus one day, he crests strongly — all owls, especially the horned ones, seem to be alarming, though this one is less than one-quarter of his weight. Later, when he has been moved to South One where we watch him from the window, he frequently comes to watch *us* and taps an inviting tattoo on the glass to catch our attention fully. But if we get too close, a rarely seen pair of eyebrow tufts rise on his crown, greatly altering his appearance. What are they signaling?

However much we enjoy the crippled raven, he cannot stay with us much longer. Winter here would be monotonous and lonely for him. Regretfully we make arrangements for him to take up residence at the Toronto Metropolitan Zoo where I am assured there is a place for him in the daily bird show for people to applaud — just his thing, I think. Ironically, he flies by plane, soaring on metal wings, without regrets; he is busily stowing away unwary knickknacks offered through the air holes of his travelling box, and has already amassed two pens, one half of a baggage ticket, seven coffee stirrers, and most of someone's lunch.

EPILOGUE

We have so far received thirteen loons that have made those mysterious dry landings. One died, but all the rest were released and two provided band recoveries. One, released in Lake Ontario in December, was found dead six months later in the same area, which told us nothing much. The other was our first land-loon whose release into Verona Lake is described in the story of "The Loon Landings." It was hunting season, and he was shot five weeks later; a friend's dog found the banded leg, which had been cut off and thrown away.

One of the four aviaries built since the writing of the book is a continuation of the Heronarium, nearly four meters high and more than doubling the space and protective foliage for the never-ending influx of immature Great Blue Herons. We had twenty-six last year alone.

Having three hundred to four hundred birds in one's house every year is sometimes inconvenient, and once, hazardous. In 1987, my autoimmune system rebelled at all the bird protein in the air, and I developed sensitivity pneumonitis, which caused scarring in my lungs. Rather than give it up, I opted to try a change, and with the help of our many supporters, a small clinic was built just opposite our back door. Now all the birds are housed and treated in the clinic, and thanks to an excellent system of ventilators (as well as occasional volunteers to help clean), I have worked in there without further lung deterioration. It is additionally pleasant that our house no longer smells of fish and mice!

Yik, now eleven years old, is still with us. Her plumage and eyes have become much darker, and her personality more rigid. Her home aviary is nearly twice as big now, and as she is both unwilling to leave it and reluctant to share it, she mostly stays home now. We now believe that when taking a captive bird for a public appearance, our verbal admonitions to leave birds alone in the wild are cancelled by a still stronger nonverbal message about our dominance over one of these creatures.

Since the overwhelming public rejection of both furs and leghold traps, we are relieved to say that we have received only a few leghold-trap victims in the last two years.

Remember how we used to have twelve to sixteen harrier chicks brought in each summer? It may well be a coincidence, but since the publication of my *Whig-Standard* column of "Bill's Way" in 1989, we have not received a single baby harrier, though we heard later of two cases in which the farmer carefully left a standing island of hay for the harrier family he wanted to protect. One of the harriers raised at the Ark without any "mousing" was brought back following a collision in April 1991. He was in his fifth year.

Wowl taught us the value of having a nesty box to sink into. Since then every aviary has one, and yes, they do get used—though so far never by two raptors at once!

GLOSSARY

Alkalosis   The acid-base balance of the body is disturbed, and body alkalinity is beyond normal. Small variations can cause death.

Bate   Ancient falconer's term for the leaping of a restrained (jessed) hawk from its perch, stump, or the falconer's fist. When on the latter, as the hawk dangles upside-down, the falconer makes a tossing movement to reseat the hawk. (It is not damaging, and somewhat resembles bungee-cord jumping!)

Brachial nerve   Main nerve of the wing.

Branching   A youngster's preflight progression from being in the nest to climbing among the branches.

Callus   Buildup of new bone where stimulated by bone damage. A callus can be felt, or seen on X-ray, forever.

Cere   Pad of soft tissue at the top of the beak.

Cloaca   The chamber that receives the terminal parts of the digestive and urogenital systems and opens to the outside. at the vent.

DMSO   Dimethylsulphoxide, a compound that penetrates skin instantly, carrying in with it any added medication; it also reduces swelling, improves local circulation, and reduces pain.

Feak   Like beak-stropping, the repeated wiping of the beak one side, then the other, on a handy branch, signalling the end of a feed. Cleaning the beak.

Follicle   Cup in the skin from which a feather develops.

Hack   Period of support during which food is provided while the free-flying bird learns wild techniques for survival (usually of falcons).

Hatch-year   Year in which a bird is hatched; a bird less than one year old. Officially all birds have a designated birthday on January 1, and are then "second-year," "after-hatch year," etc.

155

Humerus   Bone in birds and mammals between shoulder and elbow, often but not always air-filled. There are no flight feathers on this bone.

In blood   Stage of active growth of a developing feather, when it is being nurtured by an artery and vein, coloring its shaft blue.

Jesses   Used mainly by falconers. Handmade leather thongs for a raptor's legs. Jesses can be then attached to a leash on the hand or perch: this prevents the hawk from flying away.

Keel   Bony projection from a bird's sternum, much like a sailboat's keel; for attachment of major flying muscles.

Lysed   Eaten away by bacterial action; dissolved.

Mantling   A hawk standing with protectively spread wings and tail, a strong signal to other hawks of food ownership.

Metacarpal   The "hand" of the wing, from the carpal (wrist) to the tip. The largest flight feathers, called primaries, grow from this bone.

Pinning   Bone-repair operation using a temporary steel or plastic permanent insert to align two broken bone-ends. Nearly always essential for the humerus.

Radius   In birds, this is the smaller of the two bones between the elbow and wrist. Being slightly flexible, it is seldom broken in a collision.

Ringer's Lactate solution   An electrolyte solution, either oral or intravenous, to replace or balance body electrolytes.

Tarsus   The bone between the tibia and the toes. In humans it is horizontal within the foot, while in birds it is upright from the toes and is commonly spoken of as the leg, though anatomically it is not.

Toral tooth   A projection on the edge of a falcon's upper beak that fits a notch in the lower and improves the action of slicing.

Ulna   In birds, the larger of the two bones between the wrist and elbow. The large flight feathers called secondaries are attached to this bone.

METRIC CONVERSION TABLE

1 millimeter = .0394 inch

1 centimeter = .394 inch

1 meter = 3.279 feet (1.094 yards)

1 kilometer = .622 mile

1 gram = .035 ounce

1 kilogram = 2.204 pounds

1 inch = 25.40 millimeters   or
2.540 centimeters

1 foot = 305 millimeters
= 30.5 centimeters
= .305 meter

1 mile = 1.609 kilometers